SELECTIVELY LAWLESS

SELECTIVELY LAWLESS

The True Story of Emmett Long,
an American Original

Asa Dunnington

ASA DUNNINGTON

BROWN BOOKS
PUBLISHING GROUP

Selectively Lawless: The True Story of Emmett Long, an American Original

Brown Books Publishing Group
16250 Knoll Trail Drive, Suite 205
Dallas, Texas 75248
www.BrownBooks.com
(972) 381-0009

A New Era in Publishing®

Names: Dunnington, Asa.
Title: Selectively lawless : the true story of Emmett Long, an American
    original / Asa Dunnington.
Description: Dallas, Texas : Brown Books Publishing Group, [2018] |
    Includes bibliographical references.
Identifiers: ISBN 9781612542744
Subjects: LCSH: Long, Emmett. | Criminals--United States--Biography.
    | Organized crime--United States--History. | United States--
    History--1919-1933. | LCGFT: Biographies.
Classification: LCC HV6248.L785 D86 2018 | DDC 364.1092 B--dc23

ISBN 978-1-61254-274-4
LCCN 2018937718

Printed in the United States
10 9 8 7 6 5 4 3 2 1

For more information or to contact the author, please go to
www.SelectivelyLawless.com.

To Cheryl, David, Steve, and grandchildren.

FOREWORD

The Wild West provides some of the most enduring tenets of American mythology," journalist E. L. Hamilton once wrote. "And no wonder: the lawlessness of the time provided plenty of drama, and the lonely windswept territories, mountainous and arid, provided the cinematic backdrop."

True enough, but the fact is that the mythic outlaw of the frontier cannot be confined to the time and place where he first entered American popular culture. That's what we discover in the pages of *Selectively Lawless* by Asa Dunnington, the saga of a remarkable man named Emmett Long: "a rancher by profession and a gambler by passion," but also the proprietor of a speakeasy and a brothel, a bank robber, a moonshiner, a card shark, and much else besides—an authentic American original.

Born in in a small town in the Chickasaw Nation in southern Oklahoma in 1904, Emmett was one ranch hand with an early appreciation for the internal combustion engine. He'd been breaking horses since he was eight years old, but what he longed to ride at the age of sixteen was not an old paint but a motorcycle called the new Indian Scout. So Emmett was a kind of urban cowboy of the early twentieth century, even if many of his exploits recall the wildest days of the Old West.

Emmett is shown to possess exactly the kind of dangerous edge that we expect to find in a Western badman. "Heaven help the man who crosses Emmett Long," warns Dunnington. But Emmett is also a sly dog and a trickster, a man who is able to deploy a cutting sense of humor at the most awkward of moments. For that reason, Dunnington shows us scenes of jaw-clenching tension as well as scenes that make us laugh out loud, and often both at once.

Emmett may have been only a selective outlaw, but he seems to have spent a good deal of his long life on the wrong side of the law. The company he kept ranged from Pretty Boy Floyd in the thirties to Benny Binion in the sixties. Still, he turns out to be the kind of rogue whose sheer charisma we cannot help but admire. To his credit, Dunnington allows us to see Emmett's winning qualities, his kinder and gentler side, his encounters with love and loss, and his ultimate moment of redemption from his life of crime.

Dunnington first heard some of the stories "from the horse's mouth" in Emmett's old age and others from Emmett's daughter (and Dunnington's cousin-in-law), Mattie Bloomquist. Now he shares them with his reader in the engaging and compelling style of a storyteller around a campfire. And he shows us an outlaw who is unlike any of the characters we have encountered before. Emmett Long may remind us of the outlaws we meet in books and movies, but *Selectively Lawless* has the irresistible ring of the real thing.

— Jonathan Kirsch

ACKNOWLEDGMENTS

My thanks to Milli Brown of Brown Books Publishing Group for her friendship and for sticking with me through all of the legal battles it took to get here; to Katlin Stewart for keeping me on the right track; to Jonathan Kirsch and Bob Ross for helping with the legal battles; to Christy Phillippe for her friendship and editing; to Abra Myers for her photography and typing; and to Jennifer Hughes for her typing. Thanks also to my son, Steven, for keeping his foot on the pedal and to my granddaughter, Brooke, for always asking, "Is the book done yet?"

PROLOGUE

The older man and the younger man sat in the room, long shadows casting a palpable sense of heaviness and weight between them.

"It's a burden on my soul, Asa," said the older man, hunched over the table. "A burden, taking that man's life."

The younger man, Asa, nephew of the older, nodded slowly and silently, recognizing the import of what was being said, both aloud and unspoken.

"Not a day passes I don't wish it could've been different." Emmett Long, one of the so-called baddest of the bad outlaws of the old Wild West, turned in his chair to look his nephew direct in the eye.

Asa stared over at the old man, looked into the elder's clear blue eyes and saw the ring of truth behind them. He felt like a priest hearing a confession.

There was a great and profound sadness underlying Emmett's words, but the old man continued.

"You write my story for me, Asa. But don't make any excuses for me. I done what I done, and there ain't no gettin' around it."

Asa nodded.

"And if I see that fella I done kilt in the hereafter, I'll tell him the same."

And so Asa wrote the story.

CHAPTER 1

Emmett Guy Long was born in Tishomingo, Oklahoma, in the middle of the Chickasaw Nation in southern Oklahoma in 1904. That was also the year Henry Ford set a new land speed record of just over ninety-one miles an hour on a frozen lakebed in Michigan, Teddy Roosevelt was reelected president of the United States, and New Year's Eve was celebrated in Times Square for the very first time.

Tishomingo was home to less than fifteen hundred people back then, and it's barely doubled since, so most things change a lot more slowly there, as was true in the many small towns in which Emmett lived during his formative years.

He was the fourth of nine children, almost all of whom lived to adulthood, born to itinerant sharecroppers who moved from farm to farm and crop to crop, working the land with their children in exchange for food and shelter and a hardscrabble existence while attending whatever church was nearby (but preferably a Methodist one).

His father, John, would offer to preach at any church with a vacant pulpit and a hankering for a layman's stem-winder, making sure Etta Lee and the kids were all lined up in the very front pew, their faces freshly scrubbed and their clothes always homemade.

At the age of fourteen, while the rest of the family was hunkered over in a blazing Texas cotton field, Emmett suddenly rose up from the dirt between the endless rows of cotton, stretched his back, and handed his burlap collection sack to his sister Carmen.

"Carm," he said. "I picked my last."

Carmen, who was a hard worker, barely looked up. "What are you talkin' about?" She laughed before turning more serious. "Better get back to work 'fore Daddy catches you."

"I'm leavin', Carm."

"Leavin'?"

Now Emmett had his sister's undivided attention. "Next time you see me, I'll be drivin' a brand-new car with a fistful of cash in my pocket."

Before Carmen could pick her jaw up out of the dirt and respond, Emmett had stridden away, his back as straight as a carpenter's edge. He later said it was not just the backbreaking fieldwork but also the Methodist upbringing that finally got to him. "If we'd been Baptists, I'da left two years sooner."

Emmett had seen how hard his father worked to support his family and how hard the family worked in return, and he decided at a fairly young age that while the benefits of "honest labor" were many, he wasn't averse to searching out a few shortcuts on the road to prosperity.

And that road, on that day, left Pottsboro and turned due south through Grayson County, leading to his cousin Decimer Green's place. Decimer Green had a reputation in Grayson and several other counties as either a card shark or a card cheat, depending on how much the person had lost and how amenable they were to losing at cards to a woman.

The fact was that Decimer was such a good poker player that she didn't *have* to cheat, although the general rule with cards is that the better you play, the more you understand how to win—both legitimately and illegitimately.

If you want to know how to get away with murder, just ask a homicide detective.

So, Cousin Decimer took Emmett under her wing and taught him everything she knew about stud poker, draw poker, blind poker, and every other kind of poker, none of which she considered "gambling," which was lesson number one.

"Emmett," she said, "always remember: there's no such thing as gambling. There's only winning."

Well, maybe Cousin Decimer did occasionally mark a deck or two.

Emmett never forgot those words or their meaning, and for the rest of his life, he dedicated his efforts to winning as much as he possibly could, one way or another. No one he played cards with went very long before hearing him repeat Decimer's words, usually after losing another hand to him.

Emmett took to cards like a duck to water, and after only a couple of months, he rivaled his mentor in ability, so she sent him packing with an entire case of brand-new decks.

"There's only room for one of us in Grayson County," she told him, only half joking, but Emmett didn't mind.

He had plans for fistfuls of cash and brand-new cars, and he suspected those things would come a lot more quickly elsewhere than in tiny Grayson County, although later in life he'd learn there was always money to be found, no matter where you traveled.

Now he had the wherewithal; it was just a matter of where.

Emmett hit the road, hopping trains and hitching rides, taking odd jobs when he had to and making his way west, just as Horace Greeley had advised that young fella some fifty years before. He was bigger than most fourteen-year-olds but not yet the imposing figure he would later become, with a shock of thick black hair and a strong, pleasant way about him.

By the time he made Benson, Arizona, he was itching to make some real money, so Emmett checked into the nicest hotel in town, which was also the only hotel in town, Benson being little more than a rail junction between Tombstone and Tucson. But he'd seen a vast herd of cattle a few miles outside town, and Emmett was sharp enough to know that where there were cattle, there was money. He might have quit school after the third grade, but he would eventually earn a PhD in life, and that more than made up for what he'd missed in the classroom.

Emmett buddied up to the desk clerk as soon as he settled in.

"S'cuse me, sir. Can you tell me about this hotel?"

The clerk looked him up and down. Emmett seemed a little young to be on his own in a place like Benson, but he shrugged it off. "What do you wanna know?"

"You offer any extra . . . amenities?" Emmett asked innocently.

"'Amenities'?"

"You know. Food, games . . . maybe a little gambling."

The clerk gave him a sly smile. The kid was young, but he knew what he wanted. He leaned across the counter. "Got a game in back. Straight poker."

Emmett smiled. "Who plays?"

The clerk was more impressed with each question Emmett asked. "Local ranchers."

Emmett nodded. He didn't say anything for a moment, waiting for the desk clerk to offer him a spot at the table, but the older man was sharp, too. He knew better than to offer up a favor for free before it was even asked.

"Think you could get me into that game?" Emmett asked.

"I reckon I could." Unspoken was, *If you make it worth my while.*

Emmett took out a couple of bills, nearly the balance of his stash from his last job building a fence for a farmer outside Douglas. But if the game was all local ranchers, he had a feeling there would be plenty of money to replace his "entry fee."

He slid the money across the counter, and it vanished in a practiced motion so quickly Emmett figured the clerk could moonlight as a magician.

Which was a very good sign.

If the clerk was used to being bribed for a seat at the table, that meant the table was worth spending money on. On the other hand, Emmett himself could be the mark. As the saying goes among card players, "If you look around the table and don't see the sucker, that means the sucker's *you.*"

He'd soon find out.

"Tell me about these ranchers," he said.

After the clerk gave him a rundown on the various personalities who would be playing that night, Emmett went back up to his room and returned with several of his "special" decks. "When I run my fingers through my hair like this," he said, demonstrating for the clerk, "bring in these."

The clerk chuckled. *This kid is something else.* But he remained noncommittal, so Emmett slid another bill across the counter, his last, and it disappeared as quickly as the other two had. The clerk smiled. "You got it."

Emmett made sure to walk in a minute or two past seven o'clock that evening, not wanting to seem too eager and knowing the players would probably engage in a little small talk before they sat down.

Sure enough, the players were all standing around the table chatting and smoking cigars when Emmett walked in the door, immediately quieting the room. Emmett knew the moment was very important, since you never get a second chance to make a first impression.

He smiled amiably at what appeared to be a very prosperous assemblage of farmers and ranchers who had no idea the young kid who had just walked in was about to pick their pockets. "Hey there, fellers," he said. "Sorry I'm late."

One of the men laughed. "Where you from, son?"

"Emmett Long from Tishomingo, Oklahoma," Emmett answered and stuck out his hand.

The big man shook it and laughed. "We're just gettin' started," he said, and everyone relaxed. "Grab a chair, boys. Emmett Long from Tishomingo, Oklahoma, has arrived."

The big man settled in and started shuffling the cards. "Name's John Mackey," he said. "Game's straight poker." He suddenly stopped what he was doing and looked across the table at Emmett, staring intently. The entire room was silent for a very long moment. "Straight poker all right with you?"

Emmett grinned. "Looks like it's my lucky night, fellers," he blurted. "That's all I know how to play!" The entire room burst into laughter.

"Oh, we're gonna get along just fine, Emmett Long from Tishomingo, Oklahoma!"

And for the first hour and a half, they did. The winning hands were distributed fairly evenly, with Emmett watching the other players carefully without appearing to do so, memorizing their "tells," which were apparent almost immediately across the board. The big man, John Mackey, would actually give his cards a tiny nod when he had a winning hand, which told Emmett he was either none too sharp or had so much money he didn't mind losing it or both.

A quiet farmer in overalls who told Emmett to just call him "Bud" would always steal a glance at Mackey when his cards were promising, which Emmett took to mean there was some sort of personal rivalry between the two.

Sometimes the "tells" were about not just the cards themselves but personalities. A man who wanted to beat one player more than another might bet more recklessly when that player stayed in, for example, which was good to know. Emmett had a natural instinct not just for poker but for human behavior, which is what separates the good players from the great ones.

Emmett looked at the clock. A quarter to nine. He figured he'd better make a move, since farmers and ranchers would no doubt make it an early night.

He ran his fingers through his hair and glanced at the clerk.

The man was dozing in the corner!

Emmett cleared his throat and ran his fingers through his hair once more, and this time, the clerk noticed. Bud took the next pot, and the clerk leaned across the table, intercepting the old deck, which was being passed to Mackey. "You fellas about ready for another deck?"

Everyone either nodded or grunted their assent, and Emmett sat up slightly, sharpening his concentration.

A gambler never knows when he's going to win. A winner always knows, Emmett always said.

By ten o'clock, Emmett had won nearly a thousand dollars. He took care to fold early once or twice, but he won the majority of the hands for the rest of the night. He also took care never to show any emotion, no matter how large the pot.

As the game was breaking up, Mackey suddenly bellowed, "Hell's bells, Anderson, what kind of cheatin' cowboy did you let in here?" The big man was staring intently at the clerk, who, to Emmett's horror, completely froze.

Emmett knew immediately that John was playing with the clerk, basically doing the same thing to him that he'd done to Emmett when he'd stopped shuffling the cards at the beginning of the night.

The clerk was about to blow the whole thing with that guilty look on his face, and as one second of silence stretched to three and then four, Emmett knew he had to do something himself.

So, he answered the question.

"Emmett Long from Tishomingo, Oklahoma!" he said, in a passable impression of the big man's earlier exclamations.

The entire table looked from the clerk to Emmett, and then Mackey busted out laughing again, followed by the rest of the men.

"I like this kid," Mackey said. "Even though he's one lucky son of a bitch!"

As the men filed out of the room, Emmett nodded slightly to the clerk and went outside for a smoke, waving to the men as they left.

He didn't notice Mackey wasn't among them.

Emmett went back inside. The hotel was quiet, and the clerk was nowhere to be found, so he went upstairs to his room, savoring a successful night.

He unlocked his door and entered the room, which was dark except for a sliver of moonlight peeking through the tiny separation between the curtains. Emmett walked over to the bed and then froze. *Someone was in the room with him.*

"Turn around nice and slow, cowboy."

Emmett's mind worked furiously as he turned around in the darkness, assessing the distance to the window, which was unfortunately shut, and the door, which was closed as well.

Two dark figures slowly moved toward him. Emmett tensed and balled his fists. He was never one to back down from a fight, and he wasn't about to start now.

Then the light went on, and Mackey was standing there with a serious look on his face. Behind him, the desk clerk looked slightly sheepish, because he'd obviously let the big man into Emmett's room.

"You can go, Anderson."

The clerk turned and left the room quickly, not meeting Emmett's eyes.

Emmett relaxed his fighting stance and waited. He figured the big man was armed, although he didn't show it. A man like that wouldn't go up to a stranger's room, particularly a stranger who'd just cheated him out of several hundred dollars, without the odds stacked in his favor.

"I got a proposition for you, Emmett Long from Tishomingo, Oklahoma."

It just so happened that Mackey had known Emmett was cheating as soon as the decks were switched, but he couldn't figure out how, and that impressed him. Emmett accepted the compliment warily. He was pretty sure by now that Mackey hadn't come up to his room to do him harm, but he was still on guard.

When Mackey finally revealed his purpose, Emmett couldn't have been more surprised.

The big man wanted to hire Emmett as a ranch hand.

"Uh, no thanks, Mister Mackey," Emmett said. "I've had my fill of that kind of work."

The big man shook his head. "I don't want you to actually *work*, son. I want you to play poker."

The cowboys who worked Mackey's ranch typically played poker every night, and their boss had gotten an idea about how he could take back some of his payroll while watching Emmett fleece the table of ranchers, himself included.

Emmett thought about it. "How does it go?"

"I hire you on, make sure you're 'in training' with an easy job so you don't have to work too hard. You stay fresh for the games, and you win as much from those cowboys as you can. Fifty-fifty split."

"What about your men?"

"Hell, son, they'd just blow it on girls and liquor, anyway. You'll be savin' 'em from the evils of alcohol and a case of the clap!" he said, laughing.

"You can buy liquor out here?" Emmett asked. Prohibition had been passed earlier in the year.

Big John put his arm around Emmett and walked himself to the door. "Son, this is America. You can buy anything you want if you have the money. Pick you up first thing in the morning. Don't disappoint me and run off, now."

Emmett got the distinct feeling that Big John Mackey would be a little more than just "disappointed" if he didn't cooperate.

He stayed put, and for the next six weeks, Emmett "worked" all day and played poker all night, winning several thousand dollars until the well ran dry and the cowboys were ranch bound without the money to spend on liquor or women or, more importantly, gambling. So Emmett decided to take his stake even deeper into the Wild

West. This was fine with Mackey, as Emmett was leaving him with the equivalent of several weeks' free labor from his ranch hands.

"Where you headed, son?" Mackey asked.

"Always wanted to see the ocean," Emmett answered.

"California, huh? If I was a younger man, I'd tag along."

Emmett laughed at that, and Mackey joined him. They both knew there were probably lots of places not big enough for the two of them.

They shook hands, and the big man took Emmett to the bus station, and he rode out to the West Coast in style, with a fistful of cash in his pocket.

Now all he needed was a car.

CHAPTER 2

On the ride to San Diego, Emmett flipped through a magazine he'd picked up at the bus station. He wasn't that big of a reader until later in life, when he began to study the Bible, but a kindly porter had noticed him pacing while he waited for the bus to arrive and suggested he might want something to occupy his mind for the long trip ahead.

Emmett had to admit he was feeling a little anxious. He was never the sort to enjoy being cooped up for very long—something that would lead to a particularly humorous conversation some years later, when he was sentenced to Leavenworth federal prison and the guards had to continually remind him to keep his cell door closed after the evening meal.

The inmates were locked in at night, of course, but during their limited free time, they were allowed to come and go with permission, as long as they closed the cell doors when they were in their bunks and had no behavioral problems.

This was for their own protection as much as anything else, since inmates were known to have conflicts from time to time. Emmett was written up several times for leaving the door of his cell open while he napped.

"How can you sleep when somebody could sneak in there with murder on their mind?" the warden asked after hearing of his habit.

"Never met a man who scared me," Emmett answered, "but take away my freedom, and that's another matter."

The warden laughed. "But Emmett, you're in prison!"

"Maybe so, but I don't have to act like it."

Emmett thanked the man at the bus station and picked up a magazine almost at random. He waited until he was on the bus to take a better look at his purchase.

As he leafed through the pages, a particularly striking ad caught his eye. The bright red and orange colors reminded him of Oklahoma sunsets, but even more exciting to Emmett was a picture of a motorcycle and its description:

The New Indian Scout
Power! Stamina! Swiftness!

Emmett could relate to that.

If you want a mount that idles smoothly, easily, like a high-powered motorcar . . .

That gave Emmett pause. Maybe he could return home with a fistful of cash and a brand-new Indian.

. . . a machine that shoots away like the wind on an open stretch . . .

It almost sounded like one of the mustangs he'd been breaking since he was eight years old.

. . . rides as comfortably as a Pullman . . . takes the roughest roads without a murmur and the roughest use without a sign of wear . . .

That almost sounded *better* than a horse.

. . . then yours is the new Indian Scout 45! Go to an Indian dealer and climb aboard for a trial run and get ready for the thrill of your life!

That settled it. Everything in that ad appealed to a sixteen-year-old with money in his pocket and a hankering for adventure. Emmett couldn't wait to get to San Diego and buy himself an Indian.

As soon as he arrived in San Diego, Emmett checked into a hotel not far from the beach. It was an incredible thing to feel the Pacific breeze through the open window and smell the ocean a block or two away. He loved the plains, but he could see the allure of the coast as well.

Emmett went downstairs, and the desk clerk told him there was an Indian dealer within walking distance, which he took as a good sign. He rushed right over and stopped when he saw the motorcycle in the window, exactly as it looked in the magazine.

The salesman's eyes lit up when he saw the excited young man staring at the brand new Indian Scout, so he went over to introduce himself.

"Side-valve V-twin, six hundred and six cc displacement."

Emmett looked up at the salesman, who was grinning from ear to ear. He obviously had seen the advertisement Emmett had torn from the magazine and was still holding in his hand. Emmett calmly pocketed the page and waited for the rest of the sales pitch.

"Transmission's bolted right to the engine case, you know."

"That right?"

"Less rattle. Bert Roosevelt, no relation, I'm sorry to say, and this here motorized vehicle will move faster than goose crap through a cane break. It's a go-getting, wear-defying, record-setting machine you have to feel to believe, and I just know a man like you would want to climb on top and feel that power. What'd you say your name was?"

Emmett took Bert's outstretched hand. "Emmett Long."

"Well, Emmett, are you a man with a little money to spend?"

"I got me a little bit."

"How about a test ride?"

Emmett smiled. "Read my mind, Bert."

"I'll get us a couple of helmets."

When Bert returned with the headgear, Emmett was already astride the Indian. "I better sit in front, Emmett."

Emmett took off his Stetson and handed it to Bert, who shrugged and put it back inside the office. While he was inside, he heard Emmett start the motorcycle.

Bert rushed outside, and Emmett had already put on his helmet and was motioning the salesman to hop on the back. "Ever ride one of these?" Bert asked, but Emmett revved the engine and shook his head as if he couldn't hear the question.

"Let's go, Bert!" he yelled.

Emmett looked as if he were going to take off without him, so Bert quickly put on his helmet and climbed on the back.

As soon as Bert's backside hit the seat, Emmett took off like a bat out of hell, expertly navigating into traffic as Bert hung on for dear life.

"Take a left turn at the corner!" Bert screamed, but Emmett had other ideas. He sped up and swung wide around a slow-moving tin lizzie, then roared to the right, toward the ocean.

He'd been in such a hurry to find the motorcycle dealer that he hadn't even seen the water yet.

"I said left!" Bert screamed, and Emmett just nodded.

"Right!"

Emmett sped through traffic, weaving in and out of the slower-moving automobiles. Bert continued to hang on, screaming into the wind and trying desperately to get Emmett to slow down, but Emmett pretended not to hear. Emmett was having too good a time to pay attention to the man in the back.

Just as they crested a hill and the bright-blue expanse of the Pacific came into view, the sun's reflection nearly blinding, an old Model A lurched into the street from an alleyway right in front of them.

Emmett swerved into opposing traffic to avoid the collision, then hopped a curb, briefly terrorizing several pedestrians before managing to find his way back to the street in a gap between moving vehicles just as the road arrived at a cross-street dead end at the water's edge.

Emmett pulled to the side of the road and killed the engine, looking out at the wondrous Pacific Ocean for the very first time. He took off his helmet and just watched the waves for a couple of minutes before realizing his passenger had gone completely quiet.

"You can turn loose now, Bert," he said.

Bert looked down and realized he still had his arms around Emmett's waist. He peeled his hands apart and got off the Scout, his legs wobbly. "Guess you've driven one of these before."

Emmett shook his head. "First time."

Once they were back at the dealership, the negotiations went fairly smoothly. Emmett's wild ride seemed to have taken all the fight out of the salesman, and the result was a pretty good deal on the price.

After the transaction was complete, Emmett shook hands with Bert, put on his Stetson, and climbed back on the motorcycle. "How fast did you say this thing goes?"

Emmett started the engine before Bert could answer and took off like a shot, leaving the salesman slack jawed and relieved he wasn't going along for the ride.

Over the next week, Emmett rode down to the beach every day and swam in the ocean and ate Mexican food and explored Old Town San Diego, but he was eager to get back to his original plan, so he soon got packed and hit the road.

His plan was to head up the coast to Seattle on his brand-new motorcycle.

Which was not as free and easy as it sounds. This was before the construction of the Pacific Coast Highway, which would also be known as US 1, so the roads and byways along the way varied widely in quality and ease of passage. The trip took him several weeks, and by the time he crossed into Washington state, he was so beat up from the trip he couldn't wait to sell the Indian.

Emmett had spent many a day driving cattle and many a night sleeping on the ground. He'd broken mustangs and even ridden a bull or two, but his tailbone had never ached as much as it did at the end of that long trek up the Pacific coast.

In spite of the rough ride, though, he'd kept the motorcycle in good shape, and he got almost as much as he'd paid for it brand new. Good old Bert Roosevelt.

Once he'd sold the motorcycle, Emmett enrolled in barber school just long enough to become reasonably proficient, not because he wanted to actually make a living at cutting hair but because if there was one thing the logging camps throughout the region needed, it was a good barber.

And if there was one thing the camps had in abundance, it was men with ready cash in their pockets.

Emmett had no trouble at all finding a logging camp with need of his services, and he quickly contracted with the general manager to set up shop.

The loggers worked long and hard all week, and by the time the weekend arrived, they were ready to cut loose and have a good time—maybe go into town and look for girls and play a little poker on their return. So, they all wanted haircuts on Friday night, which Emmett was happy to provide. He also got himself invited to their poker games.

His situation was the same as at the ranch, only this time, he didn't actually have to work besides his barber duties, so he liked it a lot better.

Eventually, just like at the Mackey ranch, the men ran out of money to lose, and it was time once again to move on. Emmett packed up and headed to the next camp, where he cut more hair and siphoned up more wages. He kept this up until he'd basically cleaned out every logger in the Pacific Northwest, with none of them the wiser.

He figured eventually some of the loggers would either connect in town or exchange stories as they left one camp's employ for another, so he was satisfied that he'd made all the money he could as a "barber," at least for the time being.

Plus, there was that little promise he'd made to Carmen the day he left home over a year before.

Emmett went to the nearest town, found a Buick dealership, and told the salesman he wanted the sporty two-door Roadster in the middle of the showroom floor.

"Let's go see what we have in stock," the salesman said.

"Don't bother with any of that," Emmett told him. "I'll take this one."

"Actually, that one's sold. Fella's coming in this afternoon. But we have others 'round back."

Emmett reached into his pocket, pulled out a wad of bills big enough to choke a logger, and fanned out several thousand dollars. "What time did you say that other fella's comin'?"

The salesman looked down at the cash and then back up at Emmett. "What fella?"

Emmett just smiled.

Less than ten minutes later, he drove off the lot in his brand-new 1921 Buick Roadster with a canvas top and a fire-engine-red paint job that he knew his brothers would see from at least a half mile away as they hunkered down in the fields, picking cotton under the blazing southern sun.

He was smiling all the way back to Oklahoma.

CHAPTER 3

Emmett had enjoyed his adventures up and down the West Coast—especially all the money he'd made!—but the truth was that he'd gotten a little homesick, and he was ready to get back to Oklahoma to see his family. He was still just shy of his eighteenth birthday, after all. There was as much boy left in him as there was man, probably, in spite of the way he carried himself in the world.

But the eighteen-month trip had given him all the confidence in the world, and Emmett figured he could use that confidence back on familiar ground just as easily as he could out West. In a way, he felt like he'd traveled to the end of the world, and he was now convinced, like Dorothy in *The Wizard of Oz*, that after seeing all that he could see, there really was no place like home.

He passed through the same towns and dusty rail junctions that he'd seen on the way out to California, only this time, it felt different. Emmett was moving at his own pace, not depending on some stranger who'd offered him a ride or some bus schedule that didn't agree with him.

Now *he* was in charge, with no one at all to answer to, and he loved every minute of it. It felt *right* to be in control of his own destiny. When a man realizes he is in charge of the rest of his life, he wants the rest of his life to start as soon as possible.

Emmett couldn't wait to get back home and make his fortune.

It seemed that trip made him the man he was, more determined than ever to be the master of his own fate. He'd left school at the age of nine, worked in the fields alongside his father and brothers to put food on the table, and never shied away from hard work, but all that he'd experienced after leaving home had told him that a future without such an arduous path was not only a possibility—for him, it was a necessity.

The man whose father had taught him from the age of ten how to build fences with cedar poles and barbed wire for any rancher who'd hire them was not the sort of man who would be penned in by any artificial boundary, man made or otherwise.

When he passed back through Benson, he briefly considered stopping in at the hotel where he'd played poker to see if there was a game going on, but somehow he didn't think it would be the same if he pulled up in a brand-new convertible. And that's when he realized it wasn't just the money he loved; it was *winning* the money. He now understood fully what Decimer had taught him.

There's no such thing as gambling; there's only winning.

Once he'd passed through town, Emmett pulled off the side of the road to eat a sandwich he'd packed for the trip. He leaned back against the car and ate as a small group of cows gathered around a water hole a half mile away on the other side of a barbed-wire fence much like the fences he and his father and brothers had built on occasion for ranchers all across north Texas.

It was a well-built fence, with tightly strung wire and deep, solid posts. For all he knew, the land on the other side of that fence was actually part of Big John Mackey's ranch. Maybe built by the ranch hands he'd played poker with over a year ago, men who worked for another man and might spend their entire lives beholden to the property of another.

Emmett didn't want that for himself. If he'd learned anything on his Wild West adventure, it was that he needed to be his own boss.

He looked out over the flat expanse of pasture that stretched as far as he could see. He wanted to own land like that someday, to make a place where he could raise a family and where his relatives could gather. But those ranchers had it backward. They spent all week busting their backs working the land so they could relax and play poker once their work was done.

Emmett wanted to play poker all week so he could relax with his cattle after the gambling was done.

Years later, the land he was admiring in the distance would be purchased by another restless young man who'd been advised to go west: a fellow by the name of Jack Speiden, who turned the Jay Six Cattle Ranch into something of a gathering point for future politicians. A young John Kennedy was sent to the ranch with his older brother, Joe, by their father when they were just nineteen and twenty-one; later on, Barry Goldwater spent time there, too.

None of that was known to Emmett at the time, of course—not then and probably not ever. But like those other men of drive and ambition, he recognized the necessity of the land beneath his feet and felt its pull on his spirit.

His own father had been tied to the land, but it was land owned by others. Land that changed from month to month depending on where work could be found. Emmett wanted more than that. He needed more than that. There was something primal about owning the land beneath your feet, almost spiritual, and Emmett was bound to have it. He would never be tethered to land he didn't own or to a job he didn't want.

Emmett drove right up to the cotton field where his family was working, his bright-red car gleaming in the afternoon sun. Chester was the first one to reach him, but as he ran toward his brother, time seemed to almost slow down, as he couldn't quite believe what he was seeing.

Emmett had stopped off in Dallas and bought himself an expensive three-piece suit, some awfully shiny shoes, and a felt fedora that made him look like how Chester imagined the president himself would look. Emmett laughed when he saw his brother's pace slow and his jaw drop. He was leaning against his polished red Roadster, which he'd taken care to wash once he was a few miles away for maximum effect.

Chester was walking toward him now, staring at his little brother's smiling face.

Ches stopped several feet away from Emmett, staring at the man his brother had become seemingly overnight. The rest of the family was still a ways off, so the moment between the brothers was private, almost intimate.

Ches raised his eyebrows quizzically, silently asking his younger brother if he'd made good on the rest of his promise.

Emmett smiled broadly and took his hands out of his pockets. Each of his fists was stuffed with cash. Emmett nodded to his brother and replaced the money in his pockets, and the two of them fell into each other's arms, laughing hysterically. By the time the rest of the family got to them, they were rolling on the ground in the dirt next to the shiny red Roadster like a couple of children after the last school bell.

Emmett insisted they all stop working for the day so that he could buy them dinner in town. His parents' initial resistance was erased by the sight of the eighteen thousand dollars in cash he showed them, much as he'd shown Chester, by giving them a quick glimpse at the contents of the pockets of his fancy new suit.

Emmett and his family obviously had a lot of catching up to do.

The next day, Emmett went to see his friend Walter, although nobody had called him by his Christian name since he'd learned to walk. He was known as Boots from his very first steps until the day he died, because he learned to walk in, you guessed it, his father's boots. As a toddler, he rushed to put them on the moment his father took them off.

Boots had been Emmett's best friend in grammar school, and since Emmett had money to spend and a hankering to turn it into more, and since his old buddy Boots was always up for a little mischief, he figured Boots would make a good partner in whatever business the two of them could concoct to produce the largest return on their investment.

Being that this was the 1920s, the business that turned out to promise the richest reward for the least amount of work was moonshine.

Emmett remembered the words of Big John Mackey: *"Son, this is America. You can buy anything you want if you have the money."*

Which also meant that if you had what the people wanted, they would be willing to part with that money.

Now, in spite of their mutual entrepreneurial spirit and Emmett's large stake, the two of them realized they needed a little more expertise than they currently possessed to get started, so they approached an older friend, J. B., who they knew would be able to get certain materials they'd need to build the still.

J. B. had access to the copper tubing they'd need, as well as the know-how to actually build the still. Boots was in charge of the raw materials, like grain and sugar, and Emmett, being the man with the money, was responsible for bribing the right law-and-order types, who any successful bootlegger knew would be needed to look the other way from time to time.

Emmett found out who the local revenue agent was and introduced himself.

"What can I do for you, young man?"

"I was just wondering if you preferred coffee or tea in the morning," Emmett said.

The man looked at him strangely. "Why do you ask me that?"

"I figure a man who drinks coffee in the morning spends more time in the outhouse at night," Emmett said.

The man laughed. "I guess that might be so."

"And a man who spends time in the latrine at night might miss a thing or two while he's in there, from time to time."

The man's eyes narrowed. "Like what?"

"Like that sawbuck down by your feet, sir," Emmett said, pointing at the floor by the desk, where he'd surreptitiously dropped a ten-dollar bill.

The revenue agent looked down at the bill and back up to Emmett.

"If I was a betting man," Emmett continued, "I'd bet that fella down there's got a big family, all ready to come visit when the time is right."

"And what time would that be?"

"At night, after the coffee's been drunk."

The man stood up from his desk with a stern look on his face. After a moment, he walked over to his office door and closed it, then turned to face Emmett. "Fifty dollars a month for every hundred gallons, plus twenty-five a week whether you cook or not."

Emmett stood up, and they shook hands.

"And two jugs a month," the revenue agent added, "to splash in my coffee."

Emmett nodded. *This is going to be easier than I thought.*

They built the still in the woods at the base of the nearby Wichita Mountains in the game preserve area, home to bison and prairie dogs and plenty of freshwater creeks feeding Bass Lake, from which they figured they could draw as much cool, clear water as they needed to make large amounts of moonshine.

Emmett also had the brilliant idea to buy votes from the local Indians, who didn't always trust local law enforcement and so were more than willing to go to the polls and help elect the "sympathetic" sheriff of Emmett's choosing for a dollar apiece. Some of them voted several times, as a matter of fact.

Emmett Long's moonshine empire was in business, and business was good.

Then one day, Boots and Emmett decided to dynamite one of the feeder creeks to kill the fish and prepare the creek for use exclusively for their still.

They'd just set off the blast when a game warden suddenly appeared behind them out of a thick stand of trees across the water. "Where's your still?" he shouted, and Emmett instinctively drew the forty-five from his hip, spun, and fired.

The warden, his hand on his holstered sidearm, dropped where he was standing. Emmett had always been an excellent shot.

It was eerily quiet for a very long moment as Emmett and Boots just stared at the man's body, realizing the implications of Emmett's instinctual act. The man had obviously known why they were dynamiting the creek and likely could have sent them both to prison, but it was still shocking to them both.

After a moment, without a word between them, they both trudged into the woods where the still was located. They had recently leveled the ground where the still sat, and so there were shovels at the ready for what they knew they had to do.

Still silent, Emmett and his childhood friend dug the grave of the game warden, who, on closer inspection, looked no older than they were. Neither man spoke as they dug, their shirts wet with sweat by the time they'd finished the gruesome work.

Afterward, they rode home in silence, neither one speaking of what had transpired in the woods that day until Emmett confessed the deed many years later to his nephew, Asa, in the sorrowful tones of an old man looking back over a long and sometimes tumultuous life.

"At that moment, I figured it was that or prison," Emmett said. "I always regretted killin' him, and I regret it to this day. But I have to take responsibility for what I done."

Asa and Emmett sat in silence for a time, probably like the silence in which Emmett and Boots had buried the evidence of their crime.

CHAPTER 4

Emmett changed quite a bit over the years—what some folks might describe as "mellowing with age"—but with him, it was more like the older he got, the wiser he became. Part of that was just good ol' experience, of course, but Emmett was also a curious man. He had an engineer's fascination with how things worked and how to fix them when they didn't. He looked at every problem as a challenge, and he took great pride in figuring out a way to solve it. If he couldn't fix it, there was a pretty good chance it was broke for good.

That same attitude filtered into his dealings with people and his judgment of human nature. Naturally, a lot of conflicts arose in a business with criminals as its primary customer base.

You might say that he was very good at conflict resolution, because he was a fearless man who packed a mighty powerful punch. He didn't go looking to start fights, but there were plenty he finished with minimal effort.

The only time anyone ever saw Emmett truly seek out a physical confrontation was after he came back from the West Coast and went into the bootlegging business. There was a fella he'd gone to grade school with who had what he called a "runny mouth."

Emmett always took every precaution he could, which included everything from bribing the right people to look the other way to giving out a sample jug or two here and there. He figured it was just the cost of doing business, and he didn't begrudge anyone a little taste of his success from time to time. The way he saw things, his liquor went down smooth, and the business of selling it should be the same.

There could be quite a kick to both, however.

His old schoolmate with the big mouth, whom Emmett had considered a bully even as a child, had gotten into the habit of talking around town about Emmett's new business in a way that Emmett didn't cotton to.

Which is to say, talking about it at all.

But even in his outlaw days, Emmett had a code of morality based on the Golden Rule. If he was cheating at cards, he liked to win money from other gamblers who had money to lose and an inclination to cheat other people themselves. He liked nothing better than cheating a cheater.

For one thing, the gamblers who cut corners were the ones who bet the most money and so could afford to lose it. For another, the ones who cheated couldn't very well call attention to the fella who was better at cheating than they were!

On the other hand, though, in the case of illegal whiskey, there was no cheating involved at all. Emmett always gave full value for the money he was paid, since most of his customers were just working stiffs who simply wanted to take a drink without the government looking over their shoulders.

So, this loudmouth calling attention to what Emmett saw as a very lucrative public service didn't sit too well with him at all, and once it became apparent that the fella wasn't going to shut up, Emmett decided old Johnny Strange was a problem that needed to be solved.

Now, if Johnny had been a nice kid back when they were kids in school and not a bully, Emmett probably would have handled things a bit differently. That Golden Rule and all. But he remembered how Johnny, who was bigger than most of the other kids back then, used to throw his weight around. More than once, Emmett had seen Johnny push another student from behind without warning, knocking them down. Then he'd sit himself down on their back and push their face into the ground.

"You hungry?" he'd ask, laughing. "Eat some dirt!"

Emmett saw that as dirty pool, the equivalent of a sucker punch, and he had no respect for anyone who fought like that. Growing up poor with older brothers, Emmett appreciated a good fight, but he'd always hated the sneaky, unfair way bullies went about it.

Johnny had never tried that with Emmett back in the day, though. He'd known better. Since Emmett was the only kid in school tough enough to confront him, Johnny behaved himself marginally better when he was around, but the two of them had always treated each other warily, like two cautious prizefighters circling each other, trying to avoid being knocked out.

Still, that was a long time ago, and it seemed that Johnny Strange had only gotten bigger and meaner as the years passed. When Emmett returned from his trip with new clothes and a fancy car, it might have just been too much for Johnny to take.

Emmett was the talk of the town, but Johnny's talk wasn't very flattering.

More importantly to Emmett, it was downright dangerous.

In a small town, there were two kinds of secrets: the secrets that everybody knew about except outsiders, and the secrets that were taken to the grave.

In other words, everybody pretty much knew everybody else's business, but most folks had the common courtesy not to mention it in front of company.

Especially if the company could get someone thrown in the hoosegow.

Emmett went to have a talk with Johnny Strange.

He decided to take Chester as a witness. Not because he needed any backup, but because he knew Chester would enjoy telling everybody in town what had happened, and that would serve as a warning for anyone else whose lips threatened to get a little loose.

Emmett knew Chester had been dying to drive his new car, so he asked his brother if he knew where Johnny lived.

"Sure I do," Chester said, the words barely out of his mouth before Emmett tossed him the keys.

"Let's go."

Emmett didn't tell Chester why, but everybody in town knew what Johnny had been blabbing about, so he probably had a pretty good idea.

"You ain't gonna do anything stupid, are you?"

Emmett laughed. "You wanna drive or not?"

That settled it. Chester had always been the more cautious brother, which was why he'd stayed home when his younger brother, Emmett, ran off to make his fortune, but he really wanted to drive that fancy car.

Besides, he'd come to look at Emmett with new eyes after his brother's return, almost as if it were Chester who was the younger of the siblings. There was something about Emmett's adventures that had turned him into a man to be admired. He had begun to take charge of things in a way that many people never learned to do.

The brothers drove over to Johnny's parents' house, where he had ended up living his entire life.

Johnny's daddy was sitting on the old wooden porch when Chester and Emmett pulled to a stop, the cloud of dust doing nothing to lessen the effect of the shiny red vehicle silhouetted against the afternoon sun.

"How you doin', Mister Strange?"

"Tolerable, I guess," the older man answered. He craned his neck and looked at the car. After he'd had his fill, he leaned back in his rocker and gave a low whistle. "I 'spect you'll be wantin' Johnny."

"Yes, sir," Emmett answered. "If he's around."

Mister Strange chuckled. "He's around, mostly. Johnny!"

Johnny banged out of the screen door almost immediately. Emmett figured he'd been watching through the parlor window. He was tall and muscular, with a head of thick dark hair, almost a wrestler's version of Emmett.

Perhaps the WWE version.

In other words, he looked big and mean.

Chester looked nervously over at Emmett, who didn't bat an eye at the sight of Johnny.

"Remember me?" Emmett asked calmly.

Johnny sneered. It was obvious he did, but he lied anyhow. "Don't think I do."

Emmett smiled, but it didn't reach his eyes. "I reckon you will before I leave."

Johnny's smile, which had reached his eyes, faded immediately. "I'll make you eat those words."

"Come on, then."

Johnny practically leapt off the porch and charged toward Emmett, who reared back and hit him square in the jaw. Unstoppable force met immoveable object, except that, in spite of his advantage in size, Johnny was very stoppable on that day, and he dropped like a stone in the dirt.

Everybody was quiet for a moment as they waited for Johnny to stir, and when he didn't, for a moment, Chester thought he might be dead.

But then Johnny moaned, and Emmett knelt beside him. He leaned over to whisper in his ear so Johnny's father couldn't hear. There was no need to embarrass him any further.

"You hungry?"

Johnny lifted his head slightly to look at Emmett, his eyes glassy.

"Don't worry, Johnny," Emmett said. "I ain't gonna make you eat dirt."

Chester laughed.

"You thirsty?"

Johnny, still not all back with them, nodded.

"Then you're gonna have to drive over to the next county, cause I ain't gonna waste none of my whiskey on you."

Johnny's eyes cleared a little, and he finally understood.

"And if they ask why you drove so far, you go ahead and tell 'em Emmett Long sent you."

Johnny was silent. He looked completely awake now but too scared to get up for fear of being knocked down again.

"Say it."

"Emmett Long sent me."

"Damn right."

Then Emmett stood up and tipped his hat to Mister Strange, who nodded respectfully in return. The father knew his son was a bully, and everybody knew what happened to men like that. Sooner or later, they ran into somebody who wouldn't be bullied.

As Emmett and Chester walked back to the car, Johnny managed to rise up on his elbows, his legs splayed out behind him and his head in his hands, like a kid shooting marbles.

"You boys want some lemonade?"

It was Missus Strange, who'd just stuck her head out the door, completely oblivious to what had just transpired in her front yard.

Chester was about to take her up on the offer, but Emmett cut him off. "No, ma'am. We're just fine."

Chester nodded in understanding and chimed in. "Thank you, though."

"All right, then," she said cheerfully. "You boys come back anytime."

Mister Strange snorted.

Emmett and Chester tipped their hats to the mother, who, unlike Johnny's father, probably had no idea what an insufferable bully she'd given birth to. Then they got in the car, this time with Emmett in the driver's seat.

Emmett shifted into gear and drove away, shaking his head at Chester.

"Lemonade," he muttered with bemusement.

"I was thirsty."

Emmett chuckled. "You and Johnny both."

They never heard another peep out of Johnny after that day, but the general consensus around town was that from that time forward, he didn't ever take another drop of whiskey, even when it was legal again.

CHAPTER 5

The next few years for Emmett were both eventful and uneventful, meaning there was a lot going on, but it was nothing out of the ordinary for your typical entrepreneur building his small business into an ever-larger enterprise.

Emmett was amazed at just how much hard work went into being a successful criminal. He joked years later that if he'd known how much work was involved in crime, he might have gone straight a lot sooner.

"Don't believe folks that tell you crime don't pay," he'd say. "It pays pretty good if you work hard. But other things do, too, I reckon."

Emmett had seen gambling as a way to acquire money without working too hard, and that had led him into the liquor business. But the liquor business was just that, *a business,* and he was surprised to find himself a *businessman*—and a successful and well-respected one, at that.

Emmett had turned to crime in his youth to rebel against the backbreaking field labor that his father had been locked into, but lo and behold, he found himself working almost as hard outside of the fields as he had in them.

That was typical Emmett, though. No matter what he did, he threw himself into the task. It was impossible for him to be lazy or to just let things go. That was why he succeeded in everything he did, whether it was field labor or the business of selling illegal liquor. The difference now from sharecropping was, of course, that he was his own boss. Emmett believed there was something innately unfair about a man not being able to enjoy the fruits of his own labor, which was why if a man worked for Emmett, he was paid a fair wage for his efforts. Even in his criminal enterprises, Emmett always tried to be just and upright in his dealings, whether it was with a customer or a confederate.

But heaven help the man who crossed Emmett Long the wrong way.

Through the years he was in business, Emmett was always coming up with innovative ways to grow his moonshining operation, making deals with vendors for the bulk purchase of bottles, five-gallon cans, and other necessary supplies. He bought trucks for transport and votes for protection.

The Indian votes he bought for a dollar apiece turned out to be a very successful investment in democracy, successfully allowing him to place in office a sheriff who was, as they say, "no teetotaler." The new sheriff looked the other way whenever a truckload of whiskey rolled by, and he gave Emmett a heads-up whenever he saw one of those "revenuers" anywhere nearby.

Emmett even consulted with a respected Comanche medicine man he nicknamed "Big Talker." Big Talker was legendary far and wide among his people for his prophetic visions. Some said he'd even helped Pretty Boy Floyd—a gangster whom Emmett would later meet and befriend—avoid capture once or twice, but no one ever offered any proof of Big Talker's assistance.

Emmett's consultations with the medicine man may have been more political than spiritual, but they spoke regularly about the movements and actions of local law enforcement, and more often than not, the advice came in pretty handy. Either way, Emmett was too smart not to cultivate friendships that could be helpful to him and his business. At the same time, he also genuinely liked Big Talker, and they had many conversations about things other than the whiskey he provided at a discount to the old man.

Whether the Comanche's visions were prophetic or whether the medicine man and the other members of his tribe just had a habit of keeping their ears to the ground, for eight years, Big Talker kept Emmett in the loop as to which routes his drivers should take and which ones to avoid—and for eight years, Emmett had especially good fortune in that regard. The booze flowed, and the money rolled in.

But Emmett was always hungry for more, and eventually he began to see nearby Fort Sill as a huge and lucrative untapped market for his product. He knew back from his experience with the loggers that when you threw a bunch of young men together and made 'em work hard all week, they looked to cut loose on the weekends, and that usually meant a fair amount of drinking.

"You show me a hardworking fella, and I'll show you a damn good customer," he'd say, and of course, he was right.

Emmett bought a hotel in Altus, a small town with the benefit of an airstrip and proximity to Lawton, which was right down the road from Fort Sill. He turned the hotel into a speakeasy and a brothel, because the only thing those soldier boys liked as much as his whiskey were the girls who sold it, among other things, to them.

Every weekend, it almost seemed as if the entire Forty-Fifth Infantry were there, drinking and smoking and doing everything they weren't allowed to do on base, and the money continued to roll in. The base commander himself never showed up at Emmett's place, to his knowledge, but he heard through the grapevine that attendance on his property was neither officially encouraged nor discouraged, and the old man himself might have even accepted a bottle or two from Emmett's establishment from time to time.

To paraphrase Mark Twain, raising boys may be a lot of trouble, so you might as well enjoy it if you can.

Even though business was good and Emmett was mostly a genial sort, there was the occasional bump in the road that required him to travel a darker path—the darker road that Emmett had never been afraid to travel.

One morning, he was having coffee with the county sheriff—the same one who had been the beneficiary of Emmett's vote-buying strategy—when an ambitious young man in a fancy suit walked into the diner like he owned the place. It was immediately evident to anyone watching, Emmett and the sheriff included, that the man wasn't from around their parts.

First, he was dressed like he was on his way to a wedding in the middle of the week, and the area was filled with farmers and other folk who, even if they had money, normally didn't dress like it. People in Oklahoma didn't put on airs, and in Emmett's town, they were more likely to "poor mouth" themselves than to behave in a showy manner—and that included wearing Sunday clothes on a Tuesday.

Which was somewhat related to the second reason it was obvious the man was unaccustomed to the customs of the area: nobody much walked into any place like they owned it—even if they owned it. The fella's attitude was just a little too bold.

This is worth mentioning because the man's unfamiliarity with the area ended up having some pretty serious consequences, although it took a while for the whole thing to play out.

He came busting in the diner, speaking in a loud voice, basically grabbing everybody's attention like the salesman he was. Perhaps the best description of the man was how Emmett described him many years later:

" . . . like that salesman in the movie with the trombones and such," he told Asa.

"You mean The Music Man?" *Asa asked.*

"That's the one," Emmett said. "Real smooth-talkin' fella. He was selling music, too, now that you mention it."

What the brash young man was selling was actually jukeboxes, a relatively new contraption that was all the rage and something Emmett would recognize as perfect for his speakeasy.

The kid bypassed all the other customers and walked right up to where Emmett and the sheriff were sitting, which showed he was, indeed, a sharp cookie, making a beeline to the only man in town who could (a) afford to buy a jukebox and (b) had a place to put it. It was just too bad the salesman wasn't sharp enough to do a little more research and find out whom he was dealing with before he made the easiest sale of his life.

The brazen fellow sat right down with the two surprised men, immediately introducing himself and launching into his sales pitch, which Emmett took about thirty seconds to cut right off. The truth was that the kid amused him, though, besides having a product that could increase his bottom line.

Emmett took out his wallet and pulled out a wad of bills that could choke an entire rodeo. He counted out three thousand dollars, fanning the bills out in the center of the table like a five-deck dealer at Harrah's.

The sheriff noticed the young salesman's shifty eyes getting as big as saucers and the tiny smile forming at the corners of his mouth, but he said nothing. He knew better than to interrupt Emmett while he was doing business.

"I'll take two," Emmett said and went right back to drinking his coffee.

The salesman hurriedly wrote up a receipt before the rich fella could change his mind, and five minutes after he'd walked in, he was kicking up dust on his way out of town.

The sheriff waited a minute or two, but his curiosity finally got the best of him, and he asked Emmett whether he'd noticed the look in the salesman's eye when he'd laid out all that money.

"I noticed," Emmett said and took another sip of coffee.

The sheriff waited, knowing that if Emmett wanted to elaborate any further, he would certainly do so.

After a moment, Emmett grinned and stood up to leave. "Looked like me at no-limit stud." He chuckled. "He had *cajones*."

Emmett may have been laughing that day, but he wasn't laughing a few years later, when he ran into the same salesman and neither of the jukeboxes had ever been delivered as promised.

As incredible as it sounds, the salesman was having breakfast in the very same diner where he'd first approached Emmett to pitch his product. Only this time, it was Emmett who walked in like he owned the place. And Emmett's bold attitude was not driven by pride or *cajones* or greed or any of that. It was fueled by something he'd had a problem with on occasion for much of his life: one of the seven deadly sins that he'd never really learned to conquer until he gave his heart to Jesus and the one quality of his that was truly frightening to anyone unfortunate enough to be its target.

Wrath.

The very sight of the man who had so brazenly stolen his money those years before completely enraged Emmett. He walked straight over to the table, ignoring his breakfast companion, the same sheriff who'd tried to warn him about the salesman back the first time they'd met. And he placed his huge hands on either side of the plate of scrambled eggs and bacon that was soon to be as cold as the man who had ordered it.

Emmett didn't speak; he merely waited for the salesman to look up. And then the sheriff once again saw the man's eyes grow wide— but this time, it wasn't greed but fear that caused the change in his facial expression.

The lawman who had accompanied Emmett into the diner with the expectation of a nice, hearty meal, some hot coffee, and a little conversation was quite unsure what to expect at that moment. Like everyone else in town, he knew Emmett and his famous temper, and he knew better than to step in front of it without a very good reason.

A no-good, lying scoundrel of a traveling salesman was not a good enough reason.

The salesman was clearly terrified as he gradually realized just where he was and who was staring down at him, but he likely did not completely grasp just who it was that he'd stolen those thousands of dollars from.

And that was the problem from the get-go. The man had known enough to approach Emmett in order to make the sale, but he didn't know enough about the man himself.

He was about to be formally introduced.

The entire restaurant went deadly quiet. No one in the place moved or even breathed as Emmett stared down at the salesman. Many a fork hung in the air, their steaming-hot cargo turning cold, suspended inches from their digestive destinations.

Finally, Emmett spoke.

"I'm gonna ask you two questions," he said. "Answer good."

The man nodded.

"Remember me?"

The man nodded again.

"You got my money?"

The entire diner held its collective breath.

At that moment, some vestige of the bold salesman who'd barged into the very same diner years ago like he'd owned the place now somehow, terribly, bubbled back up to the surface. After having been nearly drowned in fear at the sight of Emmett leaning over the table, the man now sat up a little straighter and cleared his throat before he began what was obviously a bogus explanation.

How could you possibly explain a delivery that was nearly five years late?

"No," he said. "There was a little problem at the factory—"

Those were the last words he ever spoke, because Emmett hit the salesman so hard he literally flew back into the next booth, landing hard against the bench and then slumping over onto the table.

Emmett, all rage now suddenly drained from his system, called over to the waitress. "Eggs over easy and a side of bacon, Rosie. Black coffee, and whatever the sheriff's having."

He walked to his usual booth and sat down, not realizing for a solid minute that no one in the diner had resumed eating. No one had yet resumed anything.

"Uh, Emmett?"

Emmett looked up at the sheriff's ashen face.

"Yeah?"

"That salesman."

"What about him?"

"I think he's dead."

"Think—or know?"

Emmett looked past the lawman. The salesman did look pretty still. Emmett looked back at the sheriff and waited.

"Pretty sure he's dead."

Emmett sighed and stood up. "Guess we'd better get rid of the body."

The sheriff nodded.

"Rosie!" Emmett called.

"Yes, Emmett?"

"Make it to go."

"You got it, Emmett."

It was only then that the diner came back to life—everyone except its most recent customer, that was. Emmett and the county sheriff carried the body, and their breakfast, outside to the sheriff's patrol car.

The next day's *Lawton Constitution* carried a story on page two about a man who'd been found dead up in the foothills of the Wichita Mountains, lying right next to a peaceful creek, dead from exposure to the elements.

Heaven help the man who crosses Emmett Long.

CHAPTER 6

Even though Emmett had begun to prosper from his alcohol business, he was always looking for time when he could get back to gambling. Moonshine made him a living, but poker was his passion.

And a very good living it was, too. Besides buying the hotel he had turned into a speakeasy, Emmett began to purchase other pieces of real estate as well. Maybe because he'd grown up in a family that was forced to work on land they didn't own, or maybe because it was just a good investment, Emmett was always looking to own more property. He remembered those land-rich ranchers he'd fleeced at the poker game back in Benson, particularly Big John Mackey, who had boasted that he could get up in the morning, get on his horse, and ride all day without ever seeing the end of what he owned.

Emmett didn't know if Big John's statement came within spitting distance of the truth, but whether it was true or not, it sounded like a pretty good way to live.

Even though he had built his empire on gambling and booze, Emmett was serious when it came to making money. He always remembered his hardscrabble youth and contrasted it with those men he'd met at the poker table. They made a deep impression on him and the way he chose to live the rest of his life.

From the first days of Prohibition, there had been calls for its repeal, and Emmett figured that he should—pardon the mixed metaphor—milk that booze dry while the milking was good. He knew that the government would eventually come to its senses and realize that if folks wanted to drink, they were going to drink whether it was legal or not. Especially since all that whiskey was being bought and sold without a dime ever going to the government in the form of taxes.

Speaking of milk and whiskey, Emmett drank a lot more of the former, even when he was producing hundreds of gallons a month of the latter. He saw how alcohol could take hold of a man and make him do things he'd never do otherwise, and if there was one thing Emmett preferred, it was being in control of his own actions and of any situation in which he found himself.

He had won many a poker hand because his opponents were either drunk or on the way there, and he never wanted to make the same mistake.

Besides, he had to be sober to cheat without getting caught!

After about the age of sixteen or seventeen, Emmett never had another drop of whiskey, even though he made quite a lot of money selling it to other people. His attitude was the same as his opinion about Prohibition itself: if a man wanted to drink, he was going to drink. Legal or not. And if he wasn't buying whiskey from Emmett, he'd buy it down the road—and somebody else would be taking the money that Emmett wanted in his own pockets.

And Emmett liked his pockets full.

Yes, running a big moonshine operation turned out to be a lot more work than Emmett thought it would be, but the money was too good to give it up. In most ways, he had all the headaches and responsibilities of a traditional businessman, and as in all things that he would try in his life, Emmett became a very good businessman because he worked hard and could think fast on his feet.

Once, he was on his way down to Texas to sell a truckload of whiskey to a man who owned several dance halls in Dallas. Right before he crossed the state line from Oklahoma, one of the wheels of his truck got stuck in a muddy rut.

Emmett got out of his vehicle to work on freeing his delivery truck, and he hadn't been at it for ten minutes before an old hay truck filled with migrant workers pulled over and bought near half his load. Forty minutes and several vehicles later, and he'd sold all but a single jar, which he gave to the fella with a chain and a strong bumper who pulled him out of the mud. Emmett then went on his way with a smile as wide as the Red River.

It helped that his delivery truck was empty and his wallet was full.

But Emmett, who took his obligations seriously, still drove the truck all the way back to Cache, Oklahoma, reloaded it with the whiskey he'd promised the dance-hall owner, and headed back down to Dallas.

He managed to cross the Texas state line this time before the truck got stuck again, and that Texas mud was even more stubborn than its Oklahoma neighbor.

This time, Emmett knew to just get out of his vehicle and wait. Sure enough, the locals who drove by each bought a few jars and went off to tell their friends and relatives, and in no time flat,

Emmett had sold another truckload of whiskey by the side of the road like it was a lemonade stand, filling his wallet and lightening his load again just enough that he could push the truck out of the rut himself.

Since he knew there was no more whiskey ready to go back at the still, he drove all the way down to Dallas to tell the dance-hall owner in person that he'd have to wait a few more days for his whiskey.

"You drove all the way down here just to tell me that?" the man asked, incredulous.

Emmett looked around the room, which was filled with pretty girls who'd dance for ten cents a song. "Partly," Emmett said.

He stayed the whole weekend.

Once he got back to Oklahoma, Emmett was bound and determined to fill the dance-hall owner's order. He and Boots rode their horses out to one of his stills to begin fermenting the large amount of mash they had stored at the site.

This particular still was in the middle of a stand of mesquite trees that were thick but only a few feet tall. While they were working, a sudden hailstorm settled over the area, pounding them with hard chunks of ice the size of strawberries.

If you've ever been caught in an Oklahoma hailstorm, you know it can be very intense and arrive with very little warning, both of which applied in this case.

There wasn't any shelter nearby to speak of, but Emmett quickly ducked under his horse to escape the deluge. Boots ran from bush to bush like a chicken with its head cut off, hailstones pinging off of his body right and left.

Much to Emmett's dismay, Boots very quickly had the brilliant idea to overturn one of the barrels filled with mash and climb inside of it, wasting an awful lot of time and effort but, more importantly, discarding a good portion of the whiskey order needed for the dance-hall owner.

After the storm passed, Emmett turned over the barrel, and nothing but Boots spilled out this time, looking almost as sheepish as he felt.

"That hail *hurt*," he reasoned.

Emmett just looked at him, not knowing whether to scoff or shake his head in disgust, until the two of them busted up laughing. It was another half an hour before they could get back to work on the order—which Emmett still managed to fill and deliver according to the revised schedule.

He stayed over in Texas *that* weekend, too. He figured he deserved it after all the hard work Boots had put him through.

Sure, Emmett worked hard. But when he really needed to relax, Emmett played poker.

He kept a cabin in the woods just west of Cache where he and his poker buddies would get together for a weekly game and blow off a little steam. It was a friendly group, but the pot could get pretty large on occasion, and Emmett usually offered a healthy sample of his whiskey for those players so inclined. They were all good friends, so Emmett didn't use his famous marked decks, but he figured that if their judgment was impaired by a little hooch, that was their own damn fault.

Though most of the regulars were well known to each other, on occasion one of them would bring a friend or relative along to the get-together. As long as they had money and were who they said they were, Emmett didn't mind. Any friend of Emmett's knew better than to bring someone out to the cabin they weren't willing to vouch for.

"Just as long as you're willing to trade your life for theirs," he'd joke, and it always got a big laugh around the table and a nervous look from the newbie, until he'd settled into the game and gotten to know the fellas a little better.

There was only one time when that little joke turned out to be prophetic.

One of the regulars, a fella by the name of Wilbur who'd known Emmett from childhood, brought his cousin Jack into the game one week. Jack wasn't too bright, but he was a friendly sort who didn't mind the ribbing, and after he lost quite a bit of money that night, he turned out to be quite popular.

When he showed up again the following week, it was pretty much the same story, and so when he failed to show up the week after that, good old Cousin Jack became the topic of some spirited conversation.

Everybody likes a good-natured loser.

"Where's that cousin a' yours, Wilbur? I sure liked that fella!"

"That boy was an entertaining sort. You tell him he's welcome anytime!"

"I believe he entertained me to the tune of a hundred and fifty dollars!"

And so on it went.

Wilbur took the kidding in stride, but he had no answer as to why his cousin had suddenly disappeared.

"I reckon he's took a second job to pay for all the money he's gonna lose the next time he shows his face."

As it turned out, Cousin Jack showed up again the very next week—but he didn't exactly show his face.

The regulars were right in the middle of a hand with a good-sized pot when two men burst in through the cabin door wearing masks and carrying shotguns, which they pointed at the players. The card holders sat in stunned silence as the bandits scooped up their piles of cash and dumped it all into a cotton sack.

Two minutes later, the men were gone, and the regular players were looking at each other in complete shock. No one in his right mind would have ever stolen from Emmett, especially not at his weekly poker game, but no one but a player would have ever known how to find the remote cabin.

What former player would be so stupid as to come back and steal their money at gunpoint?

Emmett looked over at Wilbur, who knew exactly what Emmett was thinking, because it was the same thing he was thinking. Everybody knew it was his Cousin Jack who'd done it—for three reasons: Jack wasn't very smart, he knew where the cabin was, and he was wearing *the exact same pair of overalls*—torn front pocket and all—that he'd worn during his two previous visits.

Wilbur hung his head. "He ain't even really my cousin, lessen you count it by marriage."

Emmett sighed, pulled out his long-barreled pistol, and left out the door in a hurry. He was a lot more familiar with the woods than Cousin Jack was, and he beat the two bandits to the road by several minutes. When the two men, both of whom had already discarded their masks, stumbled out of the woods laughing, they saw Emmett standing in the middle of the road with a sour expression on his face.

Neither one ever was heard to laugh again.

"I gave 'em a chance, Wilbur," Emmett told his friend, "but when they raised those shotguns, it was them or me."

"I understand, Emmett," Wilbur said. "I'da done the same."

They played another hour or so. Emmett was the big winner of the night, and after the game was done, Wilbur set off across the small clearing with Emmett's shovel and instructions as to where the two men could be found.

At the edge of the woods, Wilbur turned around and looked at his friends. "Wonder what I should tell Josephine?"

"Tell her Cousin Jack shoulda bought hisself a second pair a' overalls," Emmett answered.

Wilbur smiled a little at that one, then trudged off to bury his wife's cousin, a man he barely knew but whom he had vouched for with his life, grateful that Emmett was a forgiving sort, at least as long as he got his money back.

CHAPTER 7

Nobody had ever tried to rob Emmett's poker game before that night, and certainly nobody tried again afterward, either. Not because the end result was widely known; the few people who knew what happened were not the sort ever to share such a story. It was more because people who knew Emmett liked him in spite of—and sometimes because of—his fearsome and fearless reputation.

In other words, a man like Emmett was an awfully good person to know and an even better person to know if you were on his good side. You could have no better friend in your time of need than Emmett Long, and everybody knew it.

Everybody also knew he was not a man to trifle with.

There was one person at the cabin that night, however, who *did* repeat the story of Cousin Jack and his torn overalls, and it was this loose-lipped player who first brought Emmett into contact with a man widely known for an even more fearsome and fearless reputation than himself.

A man of notoriously intemperate disposition, a man who eventually became famous all over the country for the bad things he did and many he did not, and a man whom Emmett would come to call a friend:

Charles "Pretty Boy" Floyd.

No one in his right mind would have called Pretty Boy that to his face, however, no matter how unlined and boyish that face remained.

Just like no one would ever steal from Emmett Long.

Emmett and Charlie Floyd were alike in many ways. They were the same age, they each grew up dirt poor, they both decided when they were very young not to stay that way—

And neither of them ever faced a man he feared.

Charlie was raised on the opposite side of Oklahoma from where Emmett ended up, about 250 miles away from Cache in the town of Akins, near the Arkansas border. He was born in Georgia, but he had been raised in the Cookson Hills of northeastern Oklahoma, and like Emmett, he knew firsthand the backbreaking work of picking cotton from the time he was a child.

By the time Charlie's parents packed up their eight children and moved to Oklahoma, Emmett and his family had left for Texas, but the times and the ground were still just as hard if you worked the land.

When Emmett walked out of the cotton fields to make his fortune playing poker, Charlie Floyd was still in school, a popular athlete by all accounts who played basketball and ran track.

But that, as everyone knows, was soon to change.

By the time Emmett came back home, a prodigal son with pockets full of cash and a brand-new convertible, Charles "Pretty Boy" Floyd had left Oklahoma to hire himself out as a farmhand in Missouri before migrating to St. Louis, which was where he fell in with what proud parents of wayward children typically call the "wrong crowd."

By the time Emmett had built up his whiskey business during his own "Roaring Twenties," Choc—as his friends at that time called Charlie due to his affection for the illegal beer brewed by Choctaw Indians—had married, switched jobs several times, and spent four years in the Missouri State Penitentiary for his part in the payroll robbery of a Kroger store.

Charlie's son was born while he was in prison.

Not long after that, the loquacious gambler who'd "witnessed" secondhand what happened to those who stole from Emmett Long ran into an old friend he hadn't seen for ages while he was visiting his mother in Kansas City. The talkative fellow, whose name was Stu, couldn't resist the urge to tell his buddy all about the poker game, the overalls, and the unfortunate player who'd not only lost every pot but had to bury his wife's cousin in the dead of night in the hard Oklahoma clay.

Unbeknownst to Stu, his old friend was not at all the same person he'd known as a child, and he had also fallen in with the "wrong crowd."

The old friend repeated Stu's story to his former cellmate from prison, a fella he called Choc, who'd tried and failed to find gainful employment upon his release from the Missouri State Penitentiary and who'd been working as a hired gun for bootleggers up and down the Ohio River.

Choc's cellmate had found the owner of a chemical plant who'd gotten a license to distribute alcohol as a pharmaceutical company and who'd promised Choc there would be work a little closer to his home in eastern Oklahoma. But the pseudo-pharmacist had been arrested and his operation shut down, so the story about this bootlegging gambler was of particular interest to Choc's ears.

And that was how Emmett Long met Pretty Boy Floyd before he was ever public enemy number one.

Emmett sized up the two men at the table fairly quickly, as he usually did. He had a way of looking a man in the eye that either intimidated him or put him at ease, although it was more often the former than the latter, he'd found.

It didn't bother Emmett either way, but he was more likely to bond quickly with a man who felt comfortable enough in his own skin to hold his gaze without feeling threatened.

He could tell neither man was being completely truthful about his past, but that was to be expected when someone was looking for the kind of work these two were seeking. But if he really needed what they were offering, he would have chosen Charlie and not the other one. Charlie Floyd kinda reminded him of himself.

"Fellas, I'm sorry to say, I just don't need you," Emmett told them both. "We haven't had much trouble around here."

Charlie nodded as if he understood, but the other fella, the one who'd sullenly dropped his eyes when they'd shaken hands, leaned in across the table and whispered hoarsely, "You sure? Never know what might happen in a place like this."

"This ain't Kansas City, fellas," Emmett said evenly. He knew the man's mood had shifted from promising to threatening in an instant, but this kind of man was also weak. Men like this had a tendency to underestimate everything but their own courage when the chips were down. And this one was just a little too eager to prove his manhood.

Emmett sensed Charlie tense up in his peripheral, but he held the other one's eyes until he could practically see his steam turn back to water. Charlie also visibly relaxed, and then whatever moment of danger there might have been passed.

When they parted, Emmett made a point of inviting them back that night to his speakeasy, but he was looking at Charlie when he said it.

And just as he'd thought he would, Charles "Pretty Boy" Floyd showed up that night without his friend, whom he'd apparently sent packing.

The two men sat and talked for quite a while that night, trading stories of their youth in the cotton fields and beyond. Emmett told him all about the Pacific Northwest, and Charlie told Emmett all about life in prison.

"I'm never going back there, Emmett," Charlie said. "I'll die before I let anyone lock me up again."

Charlie seemed particularly impressed that Emmett didn't actually need a guy like him. Emmett's operation was running quite smoothly with Big Talker keeping tabs on which routes the trucks should take each night to avoid government agents. Combined with timely bribes of the county sheriffs, there hadn't been too much trouble at all.

Except for one especially uncompromising deputy sheriff who had gotten into the habit of wandering the woods at night after work, trying to catch one of Emmett's gang members on their nightly booze deliveries.

The sheriff had even bragged about his extracurricular activities to the other deputies, most of whom were on Emmett's payroll and willing to snitch.

Emmett shook his head. "From what I hear, this fella sounds like your friend earlier today."

Charlie laughed. He knew exactly what Emmett meant.

Before they parted, Emmett told Charlie he was always welcome around his place, and he meant it.

"My friends call me Choc," he said.

"Choc it is," Emmett said, and the two men shook hands. As Charlie turned to leave, Emmett added, "It was Stu, huh?"

Charlie laughed and turned around. "I think that was his name."

Emmett sighed. "Always somebody."

"You got a Big Talker and a little talker."

"Ain't that the truth?"

"Speakin' of problems, I could take care of that deputy fella for you."

Emmett chuckled and shook his head. "Ain't there just yet."

"At least throw a scare into him. Best way to keep a snake on the path is to beat the bushes on both sides."

"Choc, you just gave me an idea."

"Glad to help out, Emmett," Charlie said, and then he left with a promise to return.

The very next night, Emmett took Charlie Floyd's advice and started beating the bushes. First, he sent Boots on a noisy run through the woods that a dead man would have heard.

When the eager young deputy popped out of the trees to make the big arrest, all he found on Boots was a load of chickenfeed. After letting Boots go, the confused deputy followed Ed Wright through another section of woods with an empty truck that he never loaded up. Then Fonce Grady took the man on another wild goose chase, which finally caused the deputy to give up and go home—where Emmett was waiting across the road in a stand of heavy brush with his .30-06 Springfield.

A black Model A rolled up to the house, and the deputy got out to open the door to the garage. He pulled the Ford inside and cut the motor. Just as he emerged from the darkness and closed the door, Emmett fired.

And fired again.

The deputy had barely had time to react to the first shot, which split the wood over the left corner of the garage door, when the second shot hit just above the right corner.

He dropped to the ground.

Emmett kept firing.

When he was finished, Emmett walked across the road and stood over the deputy sheriff, who was lying on his stomach in the dirt with his hands over his ears. The lights had come on in the house, but no one inside had yet emerged.

"I'm thinking you should get home a little earlier starting tomorrow night, Deputy. Maybe give the wife a little pickle tickle. Start a family."

The deputy didn't move, but he definitely knew whom he was talking to. "I could do that, Mister Long."

"And make sure you keep that garage door open in case anyone drives by. So they know you're on the straight and narrow."

"Huh?"

"The right path."

The deputy was more than a little confused by that, but he quickly agreed. He still had not moved a muscle besides his mouth. "Yes, sir, Mister Long."

"All right, then," Emmett said, and he walked back to where he'd parked. As he drove away, he could see the deputy's wife rushing outside in her robe, helping her weak-kneed husband back into the house.

He'd already opened the garage door.

The deputy called in sick for the next several days, but when he finally emerged from his house to go back to work, he was amazed by the perfectly straight, horizontal line of bullet holes across the top of the garage, each one appearing to be almost the same exact distance apart.

A few years later, when the man who'd given him the idea was public enemy number one, he and Emmett shared a laugh about the ending to the story:

Almost exactly nine months to the day after the deputy dove into the dirt in front of his garage, his wife gave birth to a brand-new baby girl.

Emmett made sure to send flowers.

CHAPTER 8

At the January 1930 term of the District Court of the United States for the Western District of Oklahoma, begun and held at the city of Oklahoma City in said District, on the 6th day of January in the year of our Lord one thousand nine hundred thirty . . .

By the time Emmett Long was twenty-four years old, he was known far and wide as a young man with whom business could be done, regardless of what business you were in. Criminal enterprises all across the Midwest were aware of Emmett and his seemingly endless supply of whiskey, which they often needed for their speakeasies and brothels.

There were many other suppliers, of course, but Emmett was known as a fair dealer and someone who could meet a deadline with the promised amount of booze, almost without exception.

If Emmett promised that a hundred gallons of whiskey would roll up to your back door on Thursday evening at six o'clock, you could bet that his truck would be leaving your premises empty before six fifteen.

It was said you could set your watch by Emmett's moonshine.

But his bread and butter was the local clientele, the folks of Comanche and the surrounding counties who bought by the jar and couldn't get enough—otherwise law-abiding citizens who didn't cotton to the government telling them what they could spend their hard-earned money on and certainly not what they could and could not drink.

In other words, typical proud, patriotic Americans.

. . . the Grand Jurors of the United States of America, within and for said District, having been duly summoned, impaneled, sworn, and charged to inquire into and true presentment make of all public offenses against the laws of the United States of America, committed within said District in said State of Oklahoma, upon their oaths aforesaid, in their name and by the authority of the United States of America, do find and present . . .

Business was booming.

It helped that oil was gushing all over the state of Oklahoma, and whether a man was flush with crude or out of work, there always seemed to be a few dollars to spend on Emmett's illegal moonshine.

It also helped that he made a superior product. Emmett ran the business side of things and generally put a hand in wherever he was needed, but the master brewer of the operation was Fonce Grady.

Fonce was a true artist of the still, with a perfect sense of timing and uncanny instincts to go with his rudimentary understanding of the actual science.

He'd also left school at an early age, learning the process from his grandfather, a farmer in Missouri who'd suffered several crop failures and had turned to making moonshine to support his family during those lean seasons.

With Emmett making the business decisions and Fonce handling the still, learning and improving on his grandfather's methods, the shine was consistently the best to be found in six counties and extremely profitable.

But all good things must come to an end, and as the Roaring Twenties wound down into the Great Depression, Emmett's luck began to turn south.

Perhaps it all started the day when Emmett, Boots, Fonce, and another rascal by the name of Ed Wright decided to take a Cadillac limousine out for a ride. Boots was the designated driver of the bunch, but as they were out joyridin' through the backwoods outside of town, he rounded a blind corner on the old dirt road and ran smack-dab into a magnificent twelve-point buck. That feller smashed right into the windscreen, flew over the cab, and landed upside down in the ditch at the side of the road.

After the spectacular collision, Boots pulled over, and they all got out with their flashlights and stood, dumbfounded, over the lifeless body of the buck. They scratched their heads, wondering what to do next.

"Boots," Fonce said, "you drive like nobody's business. Nobody I'd wanna ride with again, anyway."

"Helluva buck, though," Ed added. "What we gonna do next?"

Emmett laughed. "Guess I might dress him for supper. Won't get fresher."

"He dead?" Fonce asked, cocking his pistol.

"Appears so," Emmett said. "Killed the lights, too."

Boots walked around to the front of the limousine and saw that the headlights, sure enough, were broken. "Oh well, Emmett, let's get this here buck back to my barn and see what we can do about dinner."

Boots always was fond of thinkin' 'bout his dinner.

They made it back to the garage where they'd been keeping the limousine, and Boots backed in so they'd be able to pull out the buck and start carving it up. He parked the vehicle, the men walked over to the trunk, and then Boots flicked the latch, and the lid of the trunk opened.

It was at that precise moment that the deer came back to life.

And when that buck woke up, it came to with a vengeance—and it seemed to know just who had been the author of its attempted destruction. Before anyone could do anything to stop it, the raging animal leapt from the back of the trunk and rushed headlong toward Boots, who was only able to partially shield his important parts before the great rack of the beast lifted him from the ground and sent him flying head over heels into the back wall of the garage.

It was later claimed that the buck had lifted "Boots" right out of his "boots," but that was an exaggeration. He only lost one of them in the chaos.

The chaos being the buck running around and through the garage—multiple rounds passing through, tearing the place to shreds while the four astonished men scrambled to get the door latch opened and the deer out of their business.

Despite Boots's good fortune of retaining one boot on a foot, the group's luck had indeed begun to sour.

As Emmett's operation had grown larger and more sophisticated, increasing attention from the law was inevitable in spite of Emmett's precautions and the dubious psychic abilities of Big Talker.

It seemed like every time he turned around, there was another deputy on the job or some new county attorney who'd heard of Emmett Long and had decided to make a trip through Cache to take a measure of the man.

Using his contacts, Emmett would normally get a warning before any raid actually took place so that he could move his still to avoid detection, and of course there was always the simple, direct, cash-filled handshake. But as time went by and both his operation and reputation grew, there was simply no possible way Emmett could bribe everybody he needed to look the other way.

Emmett began to be seen as a much bigger fish in the pond that was Midwestern bootlegging, and as a result, he was inevitably arrested from time to time. Typically, he would be caught with one of his drivers and a few gallons of moonshine—or at least, that was what ended up in the court files.

The truth was that Emmett maintained his friends in high places, especially the bench above and to the left of the witness box, which meant that he never did much more than thirty days in the county jail and paid a fine, which he came to see as just another business expense. He didn't like it, necessarily, but it was something that he knew had to be done every now and then.

. . . that on the 3rd day of July, 1930, at the last residence in the north-west of Cache, Comanche County, in the Western District of the State of Oklahoma, and within the jurisdiction of this Court, Emmett G. Long, Fonce Grady, and Ed Wright, whose more full, true, and correct names are to the Grand Jurors unknown, then and there being, did then and there knowingly, willfully, unlawfully have in their possession and under their control intoxicating liquor, to-wit; whiskey . . .

It was the day before the big Independence Day celebration, and everybody in Cache was looking forward to stopping by Emmett's ranch house outside of town for some free hooch and a barbecue supper followed by fireworks. Emmett was a big believer in giving back to the community, and he always enjoyed showing his friends and neighbors a good time.

The Fourth of July fell on a Friday that year, so Fonce and Boots had been busy distilling extra shine for all of the festivities on top of what would be sold and delivered to various businesses in the area for the weekend.

After the last batch of mash had been fermented and distilled, Emmett had the men pack up to move the still, since he'd seen the new assistant county attorney drive past his house the previous morning.

The man had been pointed out to Emmett in town during his first week on the job as someone whose palm would probably need to be greased, but Emmett had been so busy with preparations for the big weekend that he hadn't stopped by the county office.

If he had done so, he might not have spent the next three years in Leavenworth.

That night, Emmett, Boots, Ed, and Fonce drove out into the woods to pack up the still. It was a warm, moonless night, and their flashlights provided the only illumination as they loaded up Emmett's truck.

The plan was to move the still to the other side of the lake after the holiday weekend, but in the meantime, they would store everything in an old barn at the edge of the woods that had been empty and abandoned for years—one Boots swore he could find, no matter how dark it got outside.

"I could find that barn with my eyes closed," he claimed to nobody in particular, but Ed snorted in response.

"That I'd like to see."

"So keep yours open," Boots answered.

"How's that?" Emmett asked. They'd only scouted the barn for use the week before.

"Brung Helen Whatshername out for a little neckin' last night," Boots answered proudly. "Weren't no moon then, neither."

"Mixin' business with pleasure, as usual," Fonce said.

"Who?" Ed asked.

"Said I don't know her name."

"Hell, Boots," Emmett said. "You brought her out *here*?"

"She don't know my name neither." Boots laughed. "Told her it was Felix."

"Kinda name is Felix?" Fonce asked.

"Like the cat, palooka!"

"All right, quit your jawin'," Emmett said. "What's done is done. And since I'd like to *be done* 'fore the fireworks go off, let's finish up."

They all clambered back into the truck, and sure enough, Boots was as good as his word. He got them to the old barn in the pitch-black night with no trouble at all. They pulled the truck inside and closed the doors behind them, which made things even blacker.

Just before Emmett turned on his flashlight, though, the sound of a motor vehicle pulling to a stop outside the barn gave him pause.

"Shh," he whispered. "Keep your lights off."

They waited in absolute darkness, seeing nothing at all, just listening. Nothing was visible through the tortured wooden slats of the dilapidated barn, either.

"Who the hell is out there?" Fonce whispered, a little too loudly for Emmett's taste. He reached out and got hold of his shirt.

"Quiet," he said so softly it was barely heard by the others.

"Weren't no lights behind us. Who the hell could drive out here blind like that?"

In the darkness, three heads turned toward where they believed Boots to be, and though he could feel their accusatory eyes, neither he nor they could see a thing in that old, beaten-down barn out there on that moonless summer night.

Before anyone *inside* the barn could offer up an idea as to what they should do next, a booming voice was heard from *outside* the barn with what might be called a strong suggestion, followed by the sudden filtered headlights of a paddy wagon.

"Attention inside!" intoned the voice. "We have you surrounded. Come out with your hands over your heads."

"Listen," Boots whispered. "I say we push a couple of slats out of the back and make a run for the woods. They don't know who we are."

"Except that's my truck outside," Emmett answered.

"Somebody musta stole it."

"Inside the barn," the voice continued. "Come out peaceful, and there'll be no trouble. Ed Wright, Fonce Grady, Emmett Long"— there was a short pause, during which time the trapped bootleggers waited for confirmation of what they already had begun to figure out for themselves—"and Felix."

And so the group of men did what most men would do in that situation. They drew their weapons and fired at the problem.

This was not received well in the front of the barn, and the voice called for its men around back to either drop where they stood or join the frontal assault so as not to lose anyone in the crossfire. Then it proceeded to blast the barn with a barrage of fire that threatened to take down the aging structure.

Inside, the four bootleggers dropped to the ground—but somehow, during the ensuing shootout, a box laden with fireworks for the weekend celebration ignited in the back of the truck, and blasting caps, pinwheels, and skyrockets added both to the confusion and to Emmett's realization that the jig, such as it was, was definitely up.

The shooting stopped fairly quickly once the policemen realized they were more likely to kill each other than they were to take out the bootleggers.

In fact, several officers were already lying facedown in the dirt, their hands over the backs of their heads like it was they who were threatened with arrest and incarceration.

It was that aspect of the operation—the fact that the police had basically formed a circular firing squad—that turned the lively shootout into a peaceful surrender in the newspaper stories the next day. It would have been highly embarrassing to the voice in charge otherwise.

Boots was the only one who got away, gingerly stepping over the cowering lawmen and slipping into the dark woods beneath the glow of the impromptu fireworks display before anyone realized his good fortune.

It was later discovered that Helen Whatshername had been working with the sheriff's office two counties over, a fact that the new assistant attorney of Comanche County, the man whom Emmett had seen drive past his house the week before, had been planning to reveal as a way to curry favor with the bootlegger.

As soon as he'd arrived at his new position, everyone he met had told him that Emmett was a good man to know and an even better friend to have when the chips were down, and he'd been excited to attend the Fourth of July party at Emmett's place.

He'd thought it would be a good time for all concerned.

. . . contrary to the form of the statute in such case made and provided and against the peace and dignity of the United States of America.

Peace and dignity, indeed.

CHAPTER 9

Emmett spent an awful lot of time and effort trying to stay out of jail after his arrest, but in the end, it was all for naught. Most of the money and property he had accumulated through the sale of his bootleg whiskey was spent on lawyers over the next several months, but in the end, none of them could keep him out of prison.

He was tried alongside Fonce and Ed, but only Emmett was sentenced to hard prison time. Fonce was acquitted on all counts, possibly because he had a baby face and looked like a deer caught in the headlights most of the time—which accurately reflected his fear of the judge and jury. Ed was convicted and sent to the Comanche County Jail, where he soon developed consumption and was released early because of it.

Emmett was another story.

He was the "big fish" in that particular pond, and the combination of an ambitious Assistant US Attorney who had eyes on leaving the "assistant" part off of his next set of business cards, plus the fact that the grand jury was empaneled and the trial was held in Oklahoma City, meant that Emmett had finally run out of luck.

The book, such as it was, got heaved full force at the man who was described as the ringleader of the gang, which, of course, was exactly what Emmett had been.

Had the courthouse in Comanche County been the venue, he never would have spent a night in jail, but given the circumstances and all of the evidence presented, he might have been fortunate to receive only a three-year sentence. It turned out the revenue agent whom Emmett had been successfully bribing had decided to go into business for himself, had quickly gotten arrested, and then had turned Emmett in to save himself, which started the entire investigation.

The Assistant US Attorney was well aware of how beloved Emmett was in the community, and he also knew all about Emmett's bribery of various local, county, and even federal law enforcement officials as needed, including the star witness, so there was never a question as to where the trial would *not* be held—and that was anywhere near where Emmett laid his head at night.

Even so, many people who knew him volunteered to testify on Emmett's behalf, although many were disqualified due to their own past legal problems. As Emmett explained to his attorneys, "I serve folks on both sides of the law, but the truth is that them on the wrong side pay their tab without persuasion. It's the law-abiding criminals I gotta remind on occasion."

Still, there were witnesses on his behalf who desperately wanted to put their hand on the Bible and vouch for his character in court, but Emmett's attorneys, who knew they were fighting an uphill battle because Emmett's operation had embarrassed the government, made sure to vet them before they determined whom to call to the stand.

One particularly eager fellow who didn't make the grade had a perfectly clean background, about which he proudly boasted to Emmett's attorneys during his mock examination.

"Do you drink alcohol, Mister Jackson?"

"No, sir, I do not."

"Have you *ever* taken a drink of whiskey, Mister Jackson?"

"It warn't always illegal, was it?" Jackson answered, smiling like the cat that ate the canary.

Emmett's attorney smiled, too. "No, indeed, Mister Jackson. So I take it you have previously imbibed."

"I have to admit that's true, sir."

"But you no longer drink?"

"Not a drop."

"And when did you stop?"

"When they closed up Emmett's whorehouse," Jackson said sadly. "Ain't been no decent hooch in Cache since he got arrested."

Mister Jackson was kept off the witness list.

There were others who testified to Emmett's character because he was so beloved in the community. No one held it against him when he sold whiskey, whether they were customers or teetotalers, because he was always there to lend a hand when a friend or neighbor was in trouble. Whether it was by giving a loan or a meal or a shoulder to cry on, Emmett would always help those in need, just as he had always done.

But character was not what the jury was charged to decide, and there was simply too much evidence against him and too much resentment among those whose justice he'd evaded.

His case even got attention from J. Edgar Hoover, who sent a letter to the warden at Leavenworth asking that Emmett's picture and fingerprints be forwarded to him personally in Washington, DC.

Emmett boarded the bus to prison broke but not broken, with plenty of time to think on the ride there, which was over four hundred miles. He actually knew quite a bit about the prison from some of his outlaw buddies who had passed through Cache from time to time, one of whom had told him that if he ever found himself confined within its walls, he should quickly find the biggest inmate in the yard when he arrived and pick a fight with him.

"Why the hell would I do that?" Emmett asked.

"Cause I seen that right of yours," the man, called Shorty, said. "You could knock out a brahman bull if you was mad enough."

"Don't know why I'd be punchin' no bull—or no inmate, neither."

"Knock out the big dog, and nobody messes with you."

Emmett thought on that for a minute. "But don't that make *me* the big dog?"

"I guess it does," Shorty answered.

"So then I'm waitin' for the next fella in to take a swing at me?" Emmett asked.

Shorty considered this. "Ain't worked that part out yet."

Emmett laughed. "Lemme know when you do."

All of that was on Emmett's mind on that long bus ride and as he went through inmate processing at Leavenworth federal prison. He was never one to look for trouble, but he figured it would be a good idea to find out who the big dog was just in case it came looking for him.

Emmett was not a formally educated man, but he was always learning, and the idea of making prison as comfortable an experience as possible intrigued him. From the day he had left the cotton fields to find an easier way to make a living, Emmett had decided he never wanted to work too hard and he wanted to enjoy whatever he did. Prison was just another place to live, he figured, and it would be whatever he made of it.

So while he had no intention of starting a fight with the big dog, whoever that turned out to be, he knew that a relationship with such a powerful man among the inmates might make things easier for him, and he decided to seek the man out as soon as possible.

As it turned out, the big dog at Leavenworth had the same idea.

William K. Hale, also known as the King of the Osage Hills, had been convicted of multiple murders only the year before and sentenced to life in prison, which turned out to be the federal penitentiary in Leavenworth, Kansas.

Like Emmett, Hale had been a well-known businessman in his community, but rather than a benevolent presence, he had killed and bullied and intimidated his way into that position of prominence. He was one of the most powerful men in Osage County during the oil boom of the early part of the century, and he'd developed an unorthodox method by which to accumulate a good chunk of the millions in royalties earned by the Osage Indian tribe, each member of which was entitled to one share of the proceeds, otherwise known as a headright.

Hale's method? Murder.

The headrights could be inherited, and you didn't have to be a tribe member to own one, so Hale came up with a devious plan to enrich himself.

First, he forced his weak-willed nephew, Ernest, to marry an Osage girl named Mollie, who owned one headright. The newlyweds moved into the house of her mother, who owned four—three she'd inherited and her own share.

Not long before they were married, Mollie's sister had been shot to death under mysterious circumstances, and not long after that, her cousin had been killed the same way. The headrights were piling up as fast as the bodies, and Hale had also taken out a large insurance policy on the cousin, himself being the beneficiary.

Hale then poisoned Mollie's mother, which meant that Ernest and his new bride were suddenly a very wealthy couple, having inherited several shares of the roughly thirty million dollars in subsurface mineral royalties due under the terms of the Osage Allotment Act of 1906.

It wasn't long before the nephew's wife started feeling a little sickly herself, and Ernest started to suspect that he was probably the next one to go after Mollie.

But when Mollie's sister's house exploded, killing her and her husband and adding two more shares to the household he'd married into, Ernest *really* got nervous.

He also got the attention of the FBI, which began an investigation that eventually led to the big dog whom Emmett would face in the yard at Leavenworth Prison on his very first day there—the King of the Osage Hills himself, William Hale: cattleman, oilman, ruthless murderer.

While William Hale was busy killing roughly two dozen people over several years and terrorizing his community, Emmett had been building his whiskey business and becoming a productive member of his own.

One in the northern part of the state, and one in the south. One benevolent, one malevolent. One ruthless, one compassionate.

Both fearless.

It was not, however, Emmett who approached the big dog in the yard to implement Shorty's somewhat shortsighted plan. Rather, it was the big dog himself who decided to circumvent the typical protocol and instead sent one of his minions to start a fight with the new fish.

That would be Emmett.

Now, Emmett was well aware of who William Hale was. Everybody in Oklahoma knew that name, and probably the entire nation had heard of his murderous treachery, which had been well documented in the newspapers over the course of several trials, mistrials, and overturned verdicts. Hale even tried to have people killed *during* his trial if he thought they might testify against him.

But Emmett had no idea what Hale looked like or that he had been assigned to the same cellblock as the architect of the infamous "Reign of Terror," which even today is recognized as the focus of one of the most complicated murder investigations in the FBI's history, as well as one of the first.

All Emmett knew was that a huge fella with a nasty scar down the left side of his face took a swing at him without warning almost as soon as he walked out into the prison yard on his very first day of incarceration.

Emmett stepped to the side and unloaded that fearsome straight right that had so impressed Shorty, and just as the little fella had predicted of the hypothetical brahman bull, Scarface went down for the count.

Several inmates, who'd rushed over as if they had known in advance that a fight was going to break out, stood in a half circle around Emmett in stunned silence. He rubbed his knuckles in annoyance and looked around to see if there was anyone else he needed to worry about. He saw two of the men standing around him glance nervously across the yard to where an older man with glasses was leaning against the wall with a curious expression on his face.

Must be the big dog, Emmett thought. The guy he'd knocked out could not have been the top guy, because the top guy would not have lowered himself in such a way. As Emmett had been something of a big dog himself in Comanche County, he knew that pretenders to the throne were the ones who approached the king, not vice versa.

So Emmett walked across the yard to properly introduce himself.

He did not follow Shorty's advice to take a swing but instead simply stuck out his right hand, the hand that had just brought low the big dog's pup, and said, "Emmett Long. Sorry about your man."

William Hale liked Emmett immediately.

Emmett did not go to work for Hale in prison, though he was asked. He had no intention of replacing the man he'd decked as William Hale's prison enforcer. The two even became friends after his jaw was reset.

No, Emmett just wanted to do his time and get out of there, and even though he also became friends with William Hale, he could never completely trust a man who'd been so murderous toward Indians, whom Emmett had always respected.

Hale did become a sort of mentor to Emmett in prison, however, and as such, they formed a mutually respectful relationship that benefited them both.

Emmett generally made the best of his time at Leavenworth, never allowing himself to feel imprisoned in his soul. As he told the warden, just because he was in prison didn't mean he had to act like it. What William Hale did teach him was that there was nothing on the outside that couldn't be gotten on the inside, especially when there were always guards who could be bought.

Emmett would have figured that out on his own, of course, but it was still good to be friends with the king—even if it was the treacherous King of the Osage Hills.

Much later, after Hale was paroled over the protests of practically everyone in Oklahoma, Emmett paid him back with the courtesy of an introduction—one that would provide him a living for the rest of his days but was as simple as their own introduction had been in the yard seventeen years before.

"Bill," he said, "meet Benny Binion."

CHAPTER 10

Emmett was released on parole about three years later during the worst part of the Depression, much poorer and quite a bit wiser, determined never again to see the inside of a prison cell, which he fortunately did not.

His vow of restraint, however, applied only to the consequences of the criminal life and not necessarily to the criminal life itself.

In other words, Emmett's conversion to a godly life was still quite a ways off.

The truth was that he had not yet seen the error of his ways, only the error of getting caught, which is a common failing of the habitual criminal. Many years later, as he told his story to his nephew Asa, he would admit that he enjoyed flouting the law before he came to Christ, especially before he settled down and had a family, which he always said was exactly what he'd been missing during the wild days of his youth.

"Asa," he said, "if I'd met Merl when I was younger, I wouldn'ta done half the things I done."

Asa nodded.

"I'da lived a better life, though." Emmett paused a moment and looked at Asa, who waited for him to continue. "Be a different book, anyway." He laughed, and Asa joined him.

When Emmett was released from Leavenworth, the calming influence of his wife and child was still decades in the future, and being the restless but pragmatic fella he was, the first thing he needed to do was replenish his finances.

And he didn't wait very long to do it.

Emmett went to see his old buddy Boots, who'd pretty much been walking the straight and narrow of late. Not because he'd turned over a new leaf, but because he wasn't quite as industrious as Emmett.

"I got an idea, Boots," was all Emmett had to say to get his old friend to perk right up, however.

"I'm all ears."

"I was thinking old Katy might be due for a visit."

Boots's jaw dropped nearly to the floor. Katy was what everyone called the Missouri–Kansas–Texas rail line, or the MKT, eventually just Katy. It was basically the southern branch of the Union Pacific Railroad.

"I ain't never robbed a train before, but I guess I could give 'er a try," Boots said slowly, clearly warming to the idea.

Emmett busted out laughing, as he often did around Boots. He could just imagine what went on in Boots's imagination, the two of them riding their horses alongside that locomotive like something out of the silent movies.

"I'm not talking about the train, Boots," he said when he'd stopped laughing. "I'm talking about the depots."

Boots closed his mouth and appeared to be thinking pretty hard. It took him a minute, but when he eventually understood, a big smile spread across his face.

They were going to burglarize the train stations, which, of course, collected money for tickets all along the line, as well as selling food and sundries and dealing in all manner of other transactions, most of which included cold, hard cash. There would have been a lot of money in those depots held overnight, probably held in locked drawers and cracker-box safes that wouldn't put up too much resistance against a couple of determined thieves.

"Emmett, I do believe that's the best idea you've had in years!"

Emmett just looked at Boots until his friend remembered he'd been in jail for a few years, and then they both laughed and sat down to devise a plan to hit as many depots as they could in a single night.

If they broke into just one, who knew what kind of security would be added to the others? Best to "get while the getting's good," as Boots liked to say.

Emmett did a little investigating and decided that the route from Altus, Oklahoma, to Wichita Falls, Texas, would do just fine. It was close enough to Cache to provide a quick getaway if there was any trouble and far enough away that he wouldn't be recognized if anyone happened to see them.

Altus was the county seat of Jackson County and home to several cotton gins and numerous wholesalers, which meant there should be a good amount of money flowing through the train station.

Wichita Falls was also a county seat, with even more businesses than Altus and the likelihood of even more cash to be had.

When Emmett told Boots of the specifics, his friend turned as white as a sheet.

"You sure you want to go all the way to Altus?"

Emmett looked at Boots askance. He was normally not one to be concerned with the "where," unless it was to get directions if he needed them.

"Altus will be loaded, Boots," Emmett said. "What's wrong with Altus?"

Boots looked down at the ground for a moment. "Kinda don't like Altus."

Emmett stared at Boots. "You're gonna hafta do better'n that." The whole point of starting in Wichita Falls was to hit everything on the way back up to Altus and then head for home from the closest point on the line to Cache.

"You remember the Robison brothers?"

Emmett frowned. "George and Verne?"

"Them's the ones."

"What about them?"

Emmett didn't particularly care for the Robison brothers or the rest of their family, who lived just outside Altus and were known to be of particularly intemperate disposition. Their daddy, Buck, was especially mean, but even their mother was to be avoided if at all possible.

Emmett had caught George and Verne snooping around one of his stills on a moonless night four summers ago, after which they'd sworn up and down they were out hunting rabbits, which was the damnedest fool excuse he'd ever heard, since nobody but an idiot would hunt rabbits at night, let alone claim to do so.

Especially without rifles.

But then again, the Robison boys were not generally known for their intellect.

"Whatcha fellas gonna do if you find one, knock 'em over the head with those fancy flashlights of yours?"

Neither George nor Verne had an answer to that, but they both knew that the mention of their gear meant Emmett knew exactly what they were doing, which was looking to steal either Emmett's whiskey or his equipment for making it, neither of which was acceptable to the owner. Why they'd attempt such a thing without their weapons drawn just proved the obvious.

Emmett walked in real close and told them in no uncertain terms that he'd appreciate them finding another place to hunt. He turned and pointedly looked at his still, then back to the Robison boys, who actually weren't much younger than he was. It was just that everybody called them that on account of George and Verne looked like they could be twins and most folks couldn't tell them apart.

But Emmett could tell them apart. It was in the eyes.

He looked into Verne's, who was two years younger than George but smarter by a decade or so. "Vernon, you tell your daddy I said hello, ya hear?"

Verne smiled gratefully. He knew that was Emmett's way of giving him a warning, but he also knew there would not be a second one. Even his daddy went out of his way to stay on Emmett's good side. "I'll sure tell him, Mister Long."

Emmett chuckled. "Call me Emmett."

"The Robison boys had a little run-in with the law while you was in the bucket," Boots explained.

"And fat meat makes grease," Emmett answered. "What do I care?"

"Well, it caused quite a ruckus up there, and I'm not so sure they ain't beefed up their, whaddyacallit, 'policin.'"

"Boots, if you're gonna tell the damn story, then tell the damn story," Emmett said. "Stop nickel-and-dimin' me."

Boots shrugged. "Ol' Verne shot himself a cop."

"That don't sound like Verne," Emmett said incredulously.

"But he told 'em it was George."

"That sounds like Verne." Emmett considered for a moment. "But I don't see George puttin' up with that," he said.

"Oh, he was incap—incapac—George was out like a light."

"What do you mean?"

"He got shot, too."

The story Emmett finally got out of Boots was that George and Verne, when they couldn't steal Emmett's equipment for making whiskey, somehow found the wherewithal to find another resource and were spotted by two law-enforcement types driving through the center of town with a still in the back of the older brother's truck.

"Now *that* sounds like George," Emmett said.

Boots laughed. "I thought so, too," he said. "Least it was at night."

"Finish the damn story!" Emmett said. "I gotta hear this."

It turned out there was a car chase and a shootout right outside town, during which Verne fatally shot Deputy Sheriff Elmer Carter and wounded the police chief, Joe Whitt, who managed to get off a shot that went straight into George's chest.

While his brother lay dying, Verne told the cops that it was George who'd done all the shooting and even gave them the name of a third man in the truck who'd been smart enough to hide in the floorboards during the worst of it. But he was stupid enough to park the truck at Buck Robison's house after he drove off with the evidence when the two cops went down, leaving Verne behind on the side of the road, or, as Boots told it, "up a creek without a paddle."

The cops found the truck with the still in the back outside the elder Robison's house, along with Ernest Jackson, the third man. The two of them were sitting in the parlor with two shotguns, listening to jazz on the radio.

Buck and Ernest implicated both Robison boys, having no knowledge whatsoever of the story Verne had told about his brother.

"So Verne blamed George, and Buck blamed 'em both," Emmett marveled. "That's a family for ya."

"I'll say," Boots said. "Ernest told the cops they was headin' down to Texas to make some whiskey. Probably didn't want to step on your toes."

Emmett snorted. "Serves 'em right, then," he said.

"For making whiskey?"

He shook his head. "For worrying about another man's toes."

It didn't take long to convince Boots that there was nothing to worry about in Altus, despite the rumors of a police state. The only trouble the two of them had was a restless night watchman in Vernon, Texas, and the safe at Wichita Falls, which was bolted to the floor and required quite a bit of extra effort to get loose.

Just as Emmett planned, they replenished their coffers with cash from every depot between Wichita Falls and Altus, and when they came to their last stop, there was a little bonus waiting for them in the stationmaster's office file cabinet.

A check-writing machine.

Emmett immediately realized their good fortune, explaining to a befuddled Boots that basically they'd found a machine that could print money. The next day, he visited an old friend, C. E. Price, who just happened to be vice president of the Cache Savings and Loan.

C. E. advised Emmett as to a few hypotheticals, and soon enough, Emmett and Boots were back on the road, this time hitting every small-town general store, train depot, and other business that sold any kind of merchandise at all between Texas and Arizona.

They'd stop in just after the local banks had closed and present a check for enough over the amount of the purchase to make it worth their while but not so much that it would attract attention or be refused.

By the time they got to Coolidge, Arizona, they had all the money they needed, so they buried the machine out in the middle of a field and drove back to Oklahoma.

It wasn't until they entered the Cache city limits that Boots suggested they should have taken a different route home so they could have started all over again with those checks, but Emmett just shook his head.

"I got other plans, Boots," Emmett said.

"What's that, Emmett?"

"How'd you like to rob a bank?"

CHAPTER 11

It turned out Emmett wouldn't be robbing a bank anytime soon, however.

Within a few days of his return to Cache after his successful check-writing trip, an unexpected visitor showed up in the middle of the night to put the kibosh on his plans, at least for the time being.

"Mister Long!"

It was a hoarse whisper, but Emmett woke up immediately. He was a sound sleeper and had been known to saw a log or two, but Emmett could also wake up in an instant if the source of the nocturnal interruption was important to life or limb.

Either his or someone else's.

It was an instinctual thing, possibly honed during his time in prison, but Emmett could just about sleep through a locomotive speeding through his bedroom as long as there was no one on the train who threatened his well-being.

Emmett sat up in bed, his eyes on the open window. He glanced at the alarm clock on the nightstand.

Three thirty-two in the morning.

He climbed out of bed with the loaded .32 he kept under his pillow for just such occasions.

"Mister Long," the voice repeated.

Emmett walked over to the window and looked outside.

Pretty Boy Floyd—Choc to his friends—was back in town.

Emmett leaned on the windowsill. Floyd was standing a few feet away, grinning in the moonlight, a crutch under one arm and a Colt automatic tucked in his waistband. There was a dark stain on one leg, as if a wound were bleeding through his pants. Emmett knew better than to ask him about it; Choc would explain when he was ready.

"'Mister Long'?" Emmett wondered aloud.

"I figure when you wake a man up, you oughta show him the proper respect," Choc answered, smiling.

"Musta shot somebody important, showing up at this hour," Emmett mused.

Choc's smile faded, but only a little. He shrugged his shoulders and waited for Emmett to invite him in.

It turned out that Floyd had indeed shot someone of note: a popular Oklahoma figure by the name of Erv Kelley, a former sheriff who'd recently retired from law enforcement to run a gas station over in Eufaula.

But gas-station owners weren't immune to the effects of the Depression any more than anyone else, so the man known across the state of Oklahoma as both a fine Christian gentleman and one of the best bounty hunters ever born had come out of retirement to catch one last criminal—that being a fella by the name of Charles Arthur Floyd.

"Thought he retired," Emmett said.

"It's that damn bounty," Floyd answered, downing the shot of whiskey Emmett had poured him. "Bankers got it up to four or five thousand by now."

Emmett whistled. "Hell to be popular."

Floyd nodded. "Ain't it the truth?"

"Good thing we're friends," Emmett said and poured him another.

Choc smiled and lifted his glass. "Hope you ain't retired, Emmett."

"Not till it's legal again," he answered. "But I been thinking about branching out."

"Doin' what?"

Emmett stood up. "Let's get you someplace safe, and then we'll talk about me."

Over the next few weeks, Emmett would get the real story about the only Oklahoman Pretty Boy Floyd actually killed, as well as some advice on robbing banks from one of the world's preeminent experts on the subject.

Emmett and Floyd drove to one of his old still sites and holed up in the cabin there. It wasn't the first time Emmett had offered Floyd a place to hide out, and it wouldn't be the last, but little did they know that it would turn out to be the only time anyone actually tracked them there.

"He shot hisself?" Emmett asked incredulously.

"More'n once," Floyd answered. Then his expression turned serious. "It was him or me, Emmett."

Emmett nodded. That was something he understood far too well.

On the night in question, Choc had gone to meet his ex-wife, Ruby, and their son, Jack, at a farmhouse just outside Bixby, Oklahoma. What he didn't know was that Erv Kelley was waiting for him with two deputized farmers and a brand-new Thompson submachine gun provided by the Oklahoma Bankers Association, who were sick and tired of Floyd robbing their banks.

They especially didn't like the fact that he usually tore up all the mortgage documents he could find and sometimes even made the bankers ride on the running boards of his getaway car so any pursuing lawmen would think twice before shooting.

More than one distinguished bank president had been humbled by walking a mile or two back into town before giving a statement to the police, during which time the disadvantages of specificity were well considered.

"That's why they hate me," Floyd would say. "Cause they got their shiny little shoes dirty."

"Soon's I got out of the car, Charlie hit the lights, and the damn fool told me to drop my gun."

"Charlie" was Charles Birdsong, one of Floyd's partners in crime.

"Erv Kelley told you to drop your gun?" Emmett asked, incredulous. "I'da just shot you," he said flatly.
  "Me too!" Floyd agreed. "And I didn't even have my gun out."
  "You think that's why?"
  "Why what?"
  "Why he didn't shoot you."

"Just let me tell the story, Emmett."

Emmett chuckled. He always wanted whoever was talking to get to the damn point already.

"Tell it, then."

As soon as he got out of the car, Choc Floyd had a sense something was amiss, but he wasn't overly concerned. He actually thought that maybe Ruby hadn't arrived yet and that was why the farmhouse was dark. He knew she'd never show up with any law enforcement. At least, none that she knew about.

In the car, Charlie Birdsong, who always had been a little twitchy, turned on the headlights just as Erv Kelley stepped from behind the chicken coop about thirty feet away.

"I think the fella behind him jammed up or something, but I wasn't waiting to see if he could use a tommy. I just drew and fired at the man in the white hat. Hit him twice in the chest. Two other fellas run off."

"He was wearing that hat?"

"Wouldn't be Erv Kelley without it."

Emmett thought about things for a moment. "So, if you hit him square, and them other boys run off, who shot you in the leg?"

"That's the crazy part, Emmett. Kelley didn't fall right away, even though I swear I got him right through the heart. Musta had his finger on the trigger of the Thompson, cause it started firing into the ground, holding him up. Shot his own damn feet, from what I saw. I caught a few ricochets."

"You tellin' me Erv Kelley shot you after he was dead?" Emmett asked.

"As I live and breathe," Floyd answered.

Emmett could only shake his head in wonder. "Musta really wanted that bounty."

Over the next couple of days, Floyd and Emmett talked about Erv Kelley, banks, and making good whiskey. Emmett taught Floyd how to cheat at cards, and Pretty Boy Floyd taught Emmett the best way to enter a bank you were going to rob.

"Walk in like you own the joint. Broad daylight. Never wear a mask, and always be nice and polite to the customers. Unless they give you trouble, which they never do. Customers don't really like banks anyway, see? Or at least the rich guys who run them."

"Why?" Emmett asked.

"Why? Cause they've got more money than they do!"

"No, why broad daylight?" Emmett asked.

Choc just looked at Emmett for a moment with a puzzled expression, until Emmett busted up laughing.

"What's so funny?" Floyd demanded.

"I just realized the difference between us, Choc."

"What's that?"

"You want the fun," Emmett said. "I just want the money."

Then it was Choc's turn to laugh.

It was on the third night that they had more than one unexpected visitor—a turn of events that very nearly killed them both.

Emmett sat up. Choc was kneeling by the window, slivered moonlight streaming weakly below the bottom of the burlap sack tacked over the opening as a makeshift curtain.

He had a .45 Colt automatic in his hand.

There was a noise outside, and Choc raised the weapon to fire. Just as he pulled the trigger, Emmett grabbed his arm, and the bullet went through the roof.

Floyd spun around and pointed the gun at Emmett, who was holding his own .32 at hip level.

The two men stared at each other for a moment without speaking.

"Who knows I'm here, Emmett?" Floyd asked.

"Just one fella 'sides me, Choc," Emmett said, his voice low and even.

The two of them stood in silence for a moment, and the entire forest seemed to do the same, until—

"That you, Ches?" Emmett called out.

"Don't shoot me," Chester yelled from outside. "I'm too tired to fall down."

Choc lowered his gun, as did Emmett. They both knew what the other was thinking. Five thousand dollars was a lot of money. Enough to make some men paranoid and other men greedy.

Chester walked in the door and saw the two of them standing there, facing off across the room, their guns at their sides.

"I'm callin' it a draw," he said.

Emmett had left a note for Chester that his older brother had understood to mean where he was, although that wasn't at all what the note said.

And the very fact that the note had been left behind at all told Chester he'd better let Emmett know if anything out of the ordinary was happening in Cache, which it most certainly was.

"There's lawmen about," Chester said. "Never seen 'em before, but the word is, they're lookin' for Choc."

"I gotta get out of here, Emmett," Floyd said, standing up. "Might need a car."

"I can get you a car, Choc," Emmett said. "But I think you oughta stay here awhile. Rest that leg."

"I ain't never goin' back to prison, Emmett. What you said last night was true. I like what I do. But I hate prison more."

"Nobody knows you're here, Choc," Emmett said.

"But they know you," he answered.

Just then, there was another sound outside, like a very careful footfall. The three men froze. Emmett and Choc lifted their weapons and strode quietly to either side of the window.

Emmett looked out and saw the glint of a badge next to a tree about twenty yards from the cabin. It quickly disappeared behind a tree. He looked at Choc, who had obviously seen the same, because his gun was up and pointed at the tree.

Emmett got Choc's attention and shook his head.

Choc shook his head, too, but it was not in agreement. He turned back to the window and raised his gun to fire.

Emmett grabbed his arm.

Choc whirled to face him again, pointing his weapon at Emmett for the second time that night.

Emmett did not respond in kind but instead called out the window. "That you, Deputy?"

Chester's jaw dropped almost as quickly as Floyd's, but before either of them could react, a young man's voice responded from the woods.

"Yes, sir, Mister Long! Came to warn you 'bout some folks!"

Emmett motioned behind the door, and Floyd quickly moved there.

"C'mon out!" Emmett called and opened the front door.

The same deputy whom Emmett had convinced to stay home at night with a line of extremely well-placed shots over his garage door had also seen the new lawmen around Cache. He'd also noticed when Chester left town in a hurry. He'd put two and two together and followed him to the cabin that night.

"I just figured you might want to know there could be some folks stop-pin' by pretty soon to check on your place," the deputy said. "So if you have any . . . er, visitors . . . that are needin' privacy . . . well, you could maybe help 'em find someplace else to go."

Emmett was standing on one side of the door and Floyd on the other as the deputy spoke. He could almost feel Choc's desire to shoot the deputy right through the door.

"Appreciate that, Deputy," Emmett said. "You best head on back now."

The deputy's eyes read Emmett's, and he did not hesitate. He merely turned without another word and marched back into the woods toward the road about a mile away, where he'd likely parked.

As soon as the door was shut, Choc moved to the window and trailed the deputy with his gun. Emmett didn't grab his arm that time, but neither did he need to.

Pretty Boy Floyd held his fire.

Once the deputy had completely disappeared into the woods, Choc lowered his weapon and asked Emmett if they could speak outside.

"Anything you say to me, you can say to Chester," Emmett said.

"Fair enough," Choc answered and put the .45 in his waistband. "The last man who grabbed my arm when I had a gun in my hand don't remember much of what happened after that."

Emmett nodded.

"And the last man who ratted me out to the cops, even by acci-dent—well, he ain't around at all." Choc's eyes briefly went to Chester, who didn't seem to notice.

But Emmett did.

"I think we got it figured then, Choc," Emmett said after a moment, and Floyd nodded.

Both men understood that blood was thicker than water. And both men understood the true difference between them.

"Reckon we do," Floyd said.

Emmett looked over at Chester, whose brow was furrowed in thought. "What's on your mind, Ches?"

Chester shook his head. "Just thinkin' about that poor last fella."

Emmett and Choc looked at Chester and then back to each other. They started laughing, soon joined by Chester. "Tell him about that deputy's garage door, Emmett."

Emmett and Pretty Boy Floyd would see a whole lot more of each other over the next upcoming months, all the way up until Choc was killed in an Ohio cornfield under widely disputed circumstances.

It wasn't until then that Emmett finally robbed a bank, disregard-ing *most* of the advice he'd been given by one of the world's most famous bank robbers.

CHAPTER 12

K now a fella name a' Frank Nash?"

Emmett wasn't surprised at Choc's question. The whiskey business was booming, but it was still the kind of business where everybody knew most everybody else if they kept at it for a while. Not everybody did, of course. Some amateurs drifted in and out, depending on their circumstances. If a farmer's yield was lower than normal, he might make a little mash and sell it to bootleggers or go the extra mile, build a still out in the barn, and sell a few jugs to his neighbors if he ran short at the end of the month. There were many who'd lost their homes to the banks, and people were adapting to hard times, as people always do.

Lots of folks knew how to make whiskey in their bathtub in a pinch, although Emmett thought most of the homebrew was pretty awful. He never tried it himself, since he'd sworn off alcohol, but Chester was always game for a taste test if he was asked nicely. Or just asked. Or not even asked at all. Ches did like a drink now and then.

As far as such fledgling competition went, Emmett had his territory locked up, so to speak, and he didn't begrudge an industrious neighbor looking for a few dollars here and there to pay the bills—as long as nobody got too greedy and the whiskey wasn't good enough to lure his customers away, which it never was.

His tolerance was mostly necessitated by circumstance. The fact was that desperate times meant not only desperate measures but an awful lot of people looking to forget about both. Emmett marveled at just how much whiskey was out there and how easy it was to get.

"Ches," Emmett once said, "a two-year-old could have a jug delivered to the front pew at high noon on Easter Sunday as long as he had a dollar in his diaper."

"And I'd be proud to adopt that child as my own."

Emmett laughed. "Wouldn't be at all surprised."

Ches looked at Emmett with the serious expression he sometimes got when he was working something out in his head. "Emmett, I don't know as you're surprised by anything."

Emmett thought about that for a moment, looking much like Chester had looked just a moment before, which Ches would have found amusing if he'd appreciated irony, which he did not. Ches had always been more of a literal-type fella.

"You're probably right about that, Ches."

That conversation flashed through Emmett's mind as he looked at his old friend, whose presence reminded him of the criminal world in which they both resided—a world filled with bootleg whiskey, gambling, and illicit gains of varying degrees.

Sometimes it was a small world, indeed. A world with a lot of familiar faces: some you avoided, and some you wanted to but couldn't.

Frank Nash was one Emmett would have preferred to avoid.

In the criminal subset of bootlegging, everyone knew everyone else. The bootleggers in Kansas City knew the moonshiners in Hot Springs, who knew the rumrunners in Chicago. No one worried Emmett in particular, neither the professionals nor the amateurs. He was confident in his shine and in his own ability to protect the business of selling it, and that applied to all comers. If Emmett worried about a few jugs here and there among friends, or if he worried about the boys in Chicago moving down into his territory, he'd lie awake all night, and Emmett was a man who had slept soundly his entire life.

Frank Nash was another matter entirely.

Emmett looked at Choc, who'd shown up unannounced, as usual, and on the run, as was also usual. He was thinking of the man he'd named, this Nash fella—a man whom Emmett had done a great favor for even though he'd only met him once.

And a man who'd very nearly killed him.

"Most things ain't worth losing sleep over," he'd often say to Ches, who was always the worrier of the two brothers, ever since their time in the cotton fields.

"There's always exceptions, Emmett."

"Maybe."

"Let's see how we feel in the morning, then," Ches would say, in another instance of unintended irony.

"Well, you know him or not?" Choc asked again.

Emmett snapped out of his reverie. "Frank Nash?" Emmett repeated slowly. "I heard of him."

Pretty Boy Floyd raised an eyebrow. He looked like he wasn't sure how to take Emmett's answer. "He's heard of you, too," he said. "And he's on his way here."

Emmett just shook his head. He hadn't seen Choc since they split up after that night in his cabin, and the first words out of his mouth were about that damned Frank Nash.

"Emmett!"

William Hale, King of the Osage Hills and noted murderer of Indians and others, also known as Big Bill or the Big Man or sometimes just Boss in Leavenworth federal prison, called Emmett over from across the yard to his prime spot in the shade of the southern guard tower.

Emmett made eye contact briefly and then turned his attention elsewhere. Big Bill was like the sun; everything revolved around him, but you could get burned if you looked directly at him for too long.

He didn't really like Bill all that much, to be honest, but he tolerated him without much problem. Bill Hale pretty much ran the prison, as far as the inmates went, and Emmett was nothing if not pragmatic. He'd turned down Bill's repeated offers to take over as his enforcer, but he also received the occasional benefit that came with the Big Man's admiration. Bill reminded Emmett of another big man he'd run across long ago: the rancher, John Mackey, with whom he'd briefly gone into business cheating his employees out of their wages.

Both were the kind of men who wielded their power carefully but without respect, which was something Emmett never did. Emmett commanded the respect of others simply by virtue of the fact that he almost always knew what he wanted and could usually figure out a way to get it. But he never went out of his way to bully anyone—something that both of these "big men" seemed to enjoy doing.

Emmett preferred to live and let live whenever possible. He didn't look for trouble, but neither did he run from it.

These two seemed to like trouble, for some reason.

Emmett sauntered across the yard to where Big Bill was waiting, purposely taking his time, stopping to exchange a few words with some of the other inmates.

Emmett knew very well how to handle men like William Hale.

Give 'em an inch, and they'd take a mile, so never give 'em an inch.

Big Bill was frowning when Emmett walked up, but his expression had changed by the time Emmett took a seat on the bench beside him. He said nothing, just waited for the Big Man to speak. Emmett always dealt with Bill as if they were sitting across from each other at a poker table, never revealing anything that wasn't to his own advantage.

They sat like that for several minutes until Bill finally relented and spoke. Emmett didn't smile, but he was suitably amused. He knew it annoyed Bill that he didn't kowtow to him like everyone else in the prison, including some of the guards, but he also knew that Bill was somewhat intimidated by him, something that was only enhanced by his silence. It was akin to being dealt two aces before the flop in Texas hold 'em.

Whatever you do, don't smile.

"Got a favor to ask," Bill said. By the way he said it, Emmett knew he wasn't going to ask twice.

"I'm listening, Bill."

Emmett was the only inmate who called him Bill.

"You heard of Frank Nash?"

Emmett nodded slowly. Bill knew damn well he'd heard of Frank Nash. It was all he'd heard about when he first got to Leavenworth. Frank Nash had broken out of Leavenworth federal prison a couple of weeks before Emmett got there, although "having broken out" was not exactly what had transpired, from what Emmett had heard. Apparently, Nash had buddied up to the warden and basically just walked away when he was let outside the exterior walls. Emmett had to admire both the nerve and the simplicity of the escape, if nothing else.

"What about him?" Emmett asked.

Bill turned to Emmett and leaned in a little, which was not like him at all. William Hale was normally a person whom other people leaned in to listen to, not the other way around.

"He's breaking back in, and he needs your help."

"I wish you'd told me sooner," Emmett said, not bothering to elaborate.

He didn't need to. Choc knew of the bad blood between the two that went back to Leavenworth, although he hadn't heard it from Emmett. Emmett was not the kind of man to complain about a problem to anyone other than the person who had caused it, which was one of the reasons he and Pretty Boy Floyd got along so well.

"Sorry, Emmett," Choc said, and Emmett knew he meant it, because he'd never heard Choc say that before, not to anyone for anything. "Kind of an emergency."

Emmett nodded. With Pretty Boy Floyd, it usually was.

"He's breaking back in?" Emmett asked, incredulous.

Big Bill laughed. "That's the first time I ever seen you surprised, Emmett."

"Yeah," Emmett said and waited for Bill to continue.

"He ain't gonna stay in," Bill said. "He's just gonna lead a few lost souls to their salvation."

"What's my end of it?" Emmett asked.

"Right to it, huh?"

Emmett shrugged.

"Them keys."

Because the warden liked him, Emmett had recently been assigned to the kitchen, which was typically easy work. During deliveries from the outside, the guards would unlock a series of doors that extended down several long hallways to the exterior of the building, finally ending at a loading dock. Normally, only the trustees were allowed to bring in supplies, but there were times when nontrustees who worked in the kitchen were needed, especially if the deliveries were larger than usual.

Emmett was a nontrustee kitchen worker.

"When?"

Big Bill smiled. "Tonight."

"When's he coming?" Emmett asked.

"Tonight," Choc answered.

Emmett sighed. "Shoulda figured."

"Shoulda told me sooner, Bill."

Big Bill frowned. He wasn't used to being refused, on the outside or the inside, not even by Emmett Long.

"Can you get 'em or not?"

Emmett looked at Bill for a long time—long enough to make the older man slightly uncomfortable, which was an extremely rare occurrence.

"I reckon."

"Midnight. Check your door."

Emmett went back to his cell with a lot on his mind. He knew why Bill had asked him to cadge the keys. Because he could do it, for one thing, but also because of his habit of leaving his cell door open. All the guards knew he left his door open, and most of them had complained to the warden about it, which didn't do them any good.

If his door were discovered ajar, it would just be shut and chalked up to Emmett's usual peculiar habit.

But that was during the day. The guards always checked that the cell doors were locked at lights-out, which meant that doing anything at midnight was much riskier. As it stood now, Emmett would be out in a couple of years. If he were caught with the kitchen keys, that could add years to his sentence, with the charge of an attempted escape added to his list of crimes.

Maybe he should leave with the others.

Emmett visited the machine shop that afternoon, and by the evening meal, he'd made his decision.

Just before lights-out, the guards made their block count and walked the line, grabbing each cell door and giving it a shake to be sure each one was closed and locked into place.

When the guard came to Emmett's cell, Emmett was standing at the sink. He splashed water onto his face just as the guard checked his door, which behaved as expected.

"Bunk down, Long," the guard said, then called out, "Twelve secure!"

The guard following with a clipboard checked Emmett off the list, and the routine continued, neither man looking at much else besides Emmett, whose actions in front of the mirror had drawn their eyes at just the perfect time.

Emmett lay down to wait.

Once things had quieted down on the block, he sat up and removed from beneath his mattress the other supplies he'd borrowed from the machine shop—and got to work.

Emmett slipped out of his cell at ten minutes to midnight, carefully removing the metal clip he'd used to hold his cell door in place. He made his way to the kitchen, silently navigating to the back of the room and the first door.

There were seven of them waiting. Emmett didn't ask them how they'd left their cells, although he assumed it was similar to his own method. He didn't say anything to them at all.

He pulled out one of the wax keys he'd made in his cell. He figured each would work twice before breaking down and becoming useless.

When he opened the last door, the famed Frank Nash was waiting there, his white teeth glinting in the moonlight. Emmett had rarely seen a man smile so broadly.

"Frank Nash," he said.

Emmett nodded brusquely and stood aside as the others slipped past. One of them whispered something to Frank, whose smile quickly faded.

"Let's see those keys."

Emmett held them out for inspection.

Frank was instantly livid. "These won't last."

"Then I'll leave 'em open."

Both men knew that relocking all the doors they'd opened after they'd escaped was the "key" to being as far away as possible when dawn broke. Frank drew a gun from his coat. His finger was on the trigger. Emmett had heard he was a hothead.

He kept his eyes fixed on Frank's.

"If you can't lock those doors behind you, we'll get caught," Frank hissed. "You were supposed to bring the keys."

"And you know damn well how risky it is to hold the keys that long."

Frank stared at Emmett. He had been perfectly willing to get his men out and leave Emmett holding the bag, and both men knew it.

They also both knew that Frank had no choice but to trust Emmett at this point, since firing his weapon would get them all caught right then.

He'd heard a lot about Frank. He was ruthless, but he wasn't stupid.

Still, there was a moment when Emmett thought his temper might get the best of him, which would cost them both dearly.

Frank's smile returned, but it never reached his eyes. He pocketed his weapon and stuck out his hand. Emmett shook it.

"See you around, Emmett Long."

And then they were gone.

Emmett did manage to relock each door, and after a couple of close calls, nearly being spotted by several guards on their rounds, he slipped back into his cell. He reheated the wax and poured it down his drain very slowly, which took almost until dawn.

He wasn't sure he would have slept much, anyway.

It was one of those exceptions.

When he opened the cabin door later that night, the grin was the same, as big and forbidding as the Cheshire cat.

"Emmett Long, as I live and breathe," Frank said.

Emmett just nodded. *Not for long, the way you're going,* he thought, never realizing just how right he was.

CHAPTER 13

Frank had old Choc laughing his head off by the time he'd finished the story about Emmett and his wax keys, even though Emmett thought Choc had probably already heard it more than once.

Frank seemed like the type who milked a story like a three-armed teat puller.

Emmett had to admit, he was an entertaining storyteller. If he hadn't been involved in the daring prison escape himself, he'd probably have enjoyed hearing about it, too.

But there was something about looking down the barrel of a gun held by a man with no conscience that tended to stick in his craw a little.

Emmett wasn't scared of Frank, but neither would he ever turn his back on him.

Men like Frank were rare, even among criminals. Every thief and murderer Emmett had ever met—and he'd run across quite a few in his line of work, not to mention in prison—always had something of a conscience about *something*.

Maybe it was children or horses or old ladies with blue hair, but he'd never met a man he truly believed had no regard at all for anything that walked or crawled on God's green earth—with the exception of Frank Nash.

Even William Hale, King of the Osage Hills and killer of women and children and anybody else who got in between him and a dollar, had a softer side when it came to his family. Once or twice, when they were alone, he'd spoken of his wife with such tenderness Emmett thought he might even shed a tear, although he doubted too many others ever saw such a side of him, especially in Leavenworth.

Bill trusted Emmett, as so many others did, because there was never any artifice about him. *"You're solid, Emmett,"* the King of the Osage Hills would say. And that was true. There was just something about Emmett that inspired confidence.

To know Emmett was to trust him.

Frank Nash was the opposite.

But he could tell a great story, and he could make just about anybody smile. Anybody but Emmett, that is.

Emmett was friendly with Frank to a point, but in spite of how gregarious Frank was and how personable he could be to just about everyone he met, there was something in his eyes that bothered Emmett. Something he figured most people never saw, or those who did hadn't lived to recount it. He couldn't quite put his finger on what it was, but Emmett generally trusted his gut about things like that.

Something about Frank was just *wrong,* somehow.

A few decades later, if Emmett had continued his formal education, he might have learned a name for what his instinct was warning him about: *psychopath.*

"You know, my sister married a Long," Frank said once they'd settled in at the local café in town.

"That so?" Emmett said without much curiosity at all, which of course made no difference to Frank, who continued flapping his jaw, much to the table's entertainment. They'd been joined by another friend of Choc's, a quiet fella named Adam who Emmett knew had robbed more than a few banks with Floyd.

"Fella from Illinois, name of John Long," Frank continued. "Runs my daddy's hotel up in Hobart with my sister, Alice. Tell 'em I sent you, and they'll treat you right."

Emmett sighed. "I'll do that, Jelly."

Frank's eyes narrowed for an instant before he smiled and went back to his patter. Choc shifted his eyes to Emmett, whose eyes betrayed nothing. Frank's friends, of which Emmett was not one, all called him Jelly, supposedly because he had loved jelly beans as a kid and also because he mixed his own "explosive jelly," which he used to blow open bank safes, by dissolving gun cotton in nitroglycerin and then adding saltpeter.

"So, you know him?"

Emmett looked at Frank blankly. Frank talked so fast it was easy to miss things sometimes.

"John Long from Enfield, Illinois," Frank said. "My brother-in-law."

"Can't say as I do," Emmett said, "*Frank.*"

Frank's eyes flickered again, but once more, he smiled and kept talking. Choc stifled a laugh this time. Poker face or not, he knew now that Emmett was messing with Frank just a little bit in that laconic way of his.

Choc, who knew Frank a lot better than Emmett did and so was even more aware of how dangerous he could be, also knew there were a couple of things that had prevented Frank from challenging

Emmett the first chance he got: the fact that Emmett was Choc's friend and the fact that Emmett had absolutely no fear of Frank at all.

Choc would later confide to Emmett that he saw Jelly as a friendly but vicious dog who would remain loyal only as long as he didn't sense fear. If he ever looked in your eyes and saw doubt, that was the end of the friendship, and he'd have to be put down.

"She used to bring us hot meals straight from the hotel kitchen," Frank said proudly. "Right in the Hobart jail."

Choc nodded. "Saw it myself."

"They wouldn't have it at McAlester," Frank continued, "or Leavenworth." Then he broke out laughing so suddenly the entire restaurant got quiet and the patrons looked over, something that rarely if ever happened when Emmett was eating with one of his out-of-town friends. Everyone in town knew to give Emmett his privacy.

"What's so funny, Jell?" Choc asked.

"That's why I left prison," Frank said. "Lousy food!"

Even Emmett had to smile at that one.

After they'd eaten, the men went back to Emmett's house. They sat down around the kitchen table, and Pretty Boy Floyd finally told Emmett why he'd shown up again.

Choc and his gang were planning to rob four banks in the same day, and they needed Emmett's help.

"Four?" Emmett asked. "How's that gonna work?"

Emmett had been planning to try his hand at bank robbing after hearing so many of Choc's stories, but he wasn't too keen on his first time out being four in the same day, and he told them so.

"You need to think big, Emmett," Frank interjected before Choc could explain the plan. "Whiskey's small time."

Emmett looked at Frank, not at all amused. Choc tensed, wondering if Jelly had finally pushed Emmett too far.

"Whiskey's all right, I guess," Emmett said evenly. "Business is good." He turned his eyes back to Choc, but his attention was clearly divided. "Not sure you need another chief, seein's you got plenty of Indians."

Choc smiled. He could tell Frank was steaming at the insult, but he knew that nothing would actually happen now. That one subtle comment was basically Emmett blowing off steam, much like Frank had been doing by talking nonstop for the last twenty minutes.

"Well, that's where you come in, Emmett. It just so happens I need me another chief for this one."

It turned out that Pretty Boy Floyd had decided to retire and wanted to go out with a big payday—and a bang. Literally, since all four banks in Dallas were to be hit in one day, and they would all supposedly have safes packed with cash that would need to be blown open, which was where Frank Nash, a.k.a. Jelly, came in.

The banks were all within a mile of each other in downtown Dallas, and the plan was basically to pull off each robbery very quickly, with precise timing, each one ending with the explosion that would send local law enforcement to that particular location just a little too late. The next explosion would set off alarms that would send everyone to the next bank, and so on until the cops didn't know whether to "crap or wind their watch," as Frank put it. "It'll be as pretty as a blue-nosed mule."

Emmett had to admit Jelly knew how to turn a phrase.

"We'll have four crews of three, Emmett," Choc explained. "But the cops will think we're the same three guys."

"Why would they think that?"

"We're gonna dress exactly the same," he answered. "Pull up a scarf at the last minute so by the time anyone takes notice, it's just some guy in a long coat and a hat with his face covered up."

Emmett was surprised. Pretty Boy Floyd had never taken pains to cover his face before or really to even *plan* a bank robbery much beyond leaving someone outside with the motor running. He must've gotten the idea from someone else. Plus, that was an awful lot of men to use.

As if he'd read Emmett's mind, Choc explained further.

"You know Jim Clark, don't you?"

Emmett nodded. James Clark was a thief and occasional bootlegger who'd joined up with the Underhill Gang and robbed banks all over Oklahoma, Kansas, and Arkansas.

"Heard him and Mad Dog was sent up to Lansing."

Mad Dog was Wilbur Underhill, a particularly vicious murderer and bank robber whom the newspapers liked to call the Tristate Terror.

Frank laughed. "I'm gonna bust 'em out."

Emmett shrugged. He obviously knew better than to question Jelly's ability in that regard.

"Jim got the idea from another fella with the same name he run into by accident up in Hot Springs," Choc said.

"That'd be Oklahoma Jack, I reckon," Emmett said. Oklahoma Jack was part of John Dillinger's gang who'd previously partnered with Baron Lamm, a German fella who'd been kicked out of the Prussian Army for cheating at cards, after which he'd immigrated to the United States to apply his precise military training to the business of bank robbery. He'd shot himself in the head rather than surrender after being surrounded by two hundred cops after his final bank job.

"That's right," Choc said. "Them two Jims got to talkin' and compared notes, I guess, but they never got to try things out cause the one got sent up for robbing the bank in Fort Scott."

"So, Jim Clark number one's in the prison at Lansing," Emmett repeated.

"Yep."

"With Mad Dog Underhill."

"Yep."

"So, they got caught," Emmett said dryly.

Before Choc could reply, Frank burst out laughing again. "And they didn't even do it!" he cried gleefully. "It was the Barker boys."

"They're inside for robbing a bank they didn't rob?" Emmett asked.

"That's why I'm busting 'em out," Frank replied.

Emmett just looked from Choc to Frank to silent Adam and then back to Choc. It sounded like a big to-do that could put everyone in Lansing or across the county in Leavenworth, and that didn't sound like anything Emmett wanted to be a part of.

He liked easy money, but his bootlegging business was doing just fine, and he was in no hurry to try his hand at banks when there were so many people involved. In Emmett's mind, the likelihood of being caught in a criminal enterprise increased exponentially with each additional member, especially when the members included people like Frank Nash and Mad Dog Underhill.

"I'll give it some thought," he said.

And he did.

What he thought was that he'd rather take things a little more slowly. And that he had a much better plan to rob a bank on his own than with his world-famous, bank-robbing friend.

His idea was a lot less risky, anyway.

He was planning to tell Choc all about it when he got the news that old Jelly had indeed broken out Jim Clark and Mad Dog Underhill, along with several other inmates, this time with pistols he'd smuggled into the prison.

Even though he'd known Frank Nash was good at such things, he'd been half hoping he'd fail so Emmett could convince Choc to come in on the safer job he'd mapped out.

But before Emmett could talk to Choc about his alternative plan, working with either one of them would become a moot exercise.

Less than three weeks after Frank Nash sprung Jim number one and Mad Dog Underhill, Jelly would be shot and killed in one of the most infamous gun battles in American history: the Kansas City Massacre.

And the number-one suspect would be Pretty Boy Floyd.

CHAPTER 14

"You in?"

Emmett looked at his old friend Choc and slowly shook his head. "You know how I feel about Frank."

Choc nodded. "You ain't never said so exactly, but I reckon I figured it out."

"You going up there?" Emmett asked.

"Need him to blow them safes."

Emmett shook his head. "I know a fella can do what he does. Maybe better."

Choc raised an eyebrow. "Nobody's better'n Jelly."

"When you headin' up?"

"Gotta be tonight. Get him on the transfer."

Pretty Boy Floyd had a fella who worked for the McAlester Police Department who'd given him the inside dope on how the FBI was getting Frank back to Leavenworth. Since federal agents weren't allowed to carry guns, the McAlester police chief would accompany them to Kansas City, where police detectives from that force would then escort them all to the prison.

"I don't know why you don't just wait till he gets in and let him bust himself out again," Emmett said. "He's pretty good at that."

Choc laughed. "Need him for Dallas."

Choc was still dead set on robbing four banks in Dallas on the same day: July 4, 1933. He figured there might be a little extra confusion when he started blowing the safes if people thought it was just fireworks. He didn't want to chance waiting it out. Plus, Choc paid a lot of attention to what old Frankie Roosevelt was doing with the banks, and that very day, he'd signed another law into effect. Choc was worried the government would keep fiddling around where they didn't belong and mess up the whole works.

"Liable to be another run or something," he said. "Whole damn well might run dry."

Emmett didn't think that made much sense, but he didn't read the papers like Choc did. "I don't know about any of that," Emmett said. "But as long as the country stays dry, I figure I'll be all right."

In point of fact, old Frankie Roosevelt had already legalized beer and wine, but Oklahoma was still technically as dry as a bone in the desert in July, which meant that Emmett was still selling as much whiskey as he could produce.

"Suit yourself," Choc answered. "I'll check back 'fore we go in case you change your mind."

The next morning, all hell broke loose at the Kansas City depot, and Emmett wouldn't hear from his friend for quite some time.

A couple of months later, Emmett robbed his first bank—if you didn't count his money-printing machine, and he most assuredly did not.

Unlike his more brazen contemporaries, Emmett figured the best time to rob a bank was when there wasn't anybody around, as opposed to in broad daylight when the place was filled with witnesses. Pretty Boy Floyd and the other bank robbers he knew seemed to enjoy the actual act of robbing the bank almost as much as the money they got after doing the deed.

The only problem was breaking into the building after hours.

Well, that and actually opening the safe without the combination. But as he'd mentioned to Choc, Emmett had that part covered.

He had it covered with his old friend J. B., a colorful fella Emmett knew from his days in Leavenworth. J. B. was so colorful, in fact, that everybody in prison avoided him like the plague. Except for Emmett, that was.

What made J. B. so colorful was that he had an opinion on every subject whether he knew anything about it or not, and most of the time, he didn't. And those opinions usually came out of him in a shout because J. B. was mostly deaf on account of the fact that he'd used explosives to blow open an awful lot of bank safes—which was why he was in prison in the first place. That made him unpopular in jail, since you don't always want everybody to know your business, and J. B. was always making you repeat everything you said.

Emmett didn't mind so much, because he never felt the need to tell anyone his business anyway, least of all J. B.

As a born poker player, Emmett always held his cards close to the vest.

So, while his world-famous bank-robbing friend was on the run from the FBI before he'd gotten a chance to rob four big banks in the city of Dallas, Emmett was making plans to rob just one little bank in the Texas town of Grandview.

The plan was to break into the bank on a Saturday night, after the workweek was done, when things were quiet. The area was populated mostly by farmers whose only day of rest was the Sabbath, and so by the time anyone realized what had happened on Monday morning, Emmett and his crew would be long gone. Emmett planned to take the entire safe and open it at a secluded location outside of town where they wouldn't be disturbed.

Emmett, J. B., and Boots drove down to Grandview that afternoon and had supper at the White Spot Café. The streets were already empty, and they were the only patrons, which only encouraged them that this would be a nice, quiet job.

Then Boots saw something across the street that he thought Emmett should know about. He leaned across the table and whispered, "Looks like there's a night watchman at the bank."

Emmett turned to look, and sure enough, there was a man in uniform walking around the bank building. He turned back to Boots, and—

"There's a what at the bank?"

It was J. B., who, of course, hadn't heard much of what had been said but had managed to repeat the most revealing part.

Emmett saw in his peripheral vision that the counterman was looking up from his paper.

"The bank's not open, Grandpa," Boots said, just as loudly as J. B. "We can come back on Monday!"

They quickly finished eating and left, but it was still light outside, so Emmett drove to the outskirts of town and checked his exit route one more time. They wanted to blow the safe by dawn and be back in Cache by lunchtime.

When they got back into town, it was dark, but to Emmett's surprise, the café was still open. He figured the owner would have closed up by then, since it looked like they'd been the last customers of the night. And because the café was across the street from the bank, that presented a problem.

So much for no witnesses.

Emmett went back inside the café, followed by Boots. They left J. B. in the truck.

The counterman looked up quizzically. "Fellas forget something?"

"We did," Emmett said. "You know the night watchman over at the bank?"

"Elmer Tate?"

Emmett pulled out his .45 and pointed it at the surprised counterman. "Why don't you stick your head out there and invite Elmer over for supper?"

Once they'd tied up the two men, Emmett and his crew backed up his truck to the walkway in front of the bank. It was actually a good thing that the counterman hadn't closed up earlier, he realized, because his friend the night watchman had been very helpful with information about the brand-new alarm system that had been installed recently after a daylight robbery the month before.

"All the modern amenities!" J. B. had shouted.

They had no problem at all with the safe, which they mounted on rollers and wheeled outside just like they were picking up a laundry cart.

But what stopped them in their tracks were the hundred or so people filing out of the movie house around the corner from the café, which they'd somehow missed on their way into town, maybe because the marquee hadn't been all lit up like it was now.

"*King Kong*!" J. B. shouted, reading the brightly lit neon sign. "I been wanting to see that!"

As the people walked by them standing there next to their truck with the bank safe on rollers, to Emmett's astonishment, no one paid them any mind at all. Either *King Kong* was one engrossing movie or nobody much cared if you robbed the town's bank.

Emmett figured later that it was probably both, as bankers were not very well liked during the Depression, and he went to see the movie for himself the very next week, although not at that particular theater.

"You fellas need a hand?"

Emmett turned to see a big man in overalls, probably a farmer, eyeing the safe and the back of the truck and calculating that a fourth set of hands would probably be helpful.

"Say what?" J. B. shouted.

Emmett nudged his old prison buddy toward one corner of the safe he'd soon be opening and nodded to the man in the overalls. "Much obliged."

The four of them lifted the safe onto the bed of the truck, and the Good Samaritan even shook their hands before continuing on his way. Emmett saw that the line at the café was looking pretty long, so he knew why the counterman had stayed open so late and why they'd better get out of town pretty quick. Any minute now, one of those hungry moviegoers would check in the back room, and that watchman probably wouldn't be as charitable as the man in overalls.

They drove on out of town.

Once they arrived at the designated spot, they offloaded the safe, and J. B. went to work. He placed two sticks of dynamite next to the hinges and lit a very long fuse, then ran like hell to where Emmett and Boots were waiting.

And they waited.

And waited.

"What's the holdup?" Boots asked.

Just then, the loudest explosion Emmett had heard since his logging days filled the air around them with rocks and dirt.

J. B. turned to Boots. "What's the *what*?"

They rushed over to the safe, and to their surprise, it was completely intact. It looked even better than it had before, if that were possible, because the blast had blown all the road dust off.

J. B. shook his head. "Better mix up some jelly!" he shouted.

They waited while J. B. went to his old satchel and took out the ingredients to make nitroglycerin. By the time he'd finished, it was dawn, but this time, the safe jumped about twenty feet in the air and came down without its door, showering them with cash and securities.

Emmett and the others went scrambling to collect all the cash, and Emmett made sure they collected all the miscellaneous papers as well.

"Why do we want them papers?" J. B. asked.

"Just get everything."

"Just *what*?"

After they split up the cash and went their separate ways, Emmett took all the mortgages and such that had been stored in the safe and burnt them with the trash, just like his old friend Pretty Boy Floyd would have done.

He only hoped the Good Samaritan's had been among them.

CHAPTER 15

Heard that was Clyde Barrow," Choc said.

Emmett shrugged. "Maybe it was," he said.

Choc laughed. Emmett had just told him all about the bank in Grandview and was surprised that his friend had already heard about it, albeit with a very different narrative.

"You're a cool customer, Emmett."

Emmett just smiled.

"They say you cut into the safe right there in the bank."

"You mean Clyde."

Choc laughed again. "They say he torched a hole in the top while Bonnie pistol-whipped the night watchman."

Emmett just shook his head. *That makes a better story than getting hogtied next to a bag of flour.* "Folks like to talk."

"Indeed they do."

Emmett could tell Choc couldn't quite figure him out sometimes, and that was fine with him. The minute that people figured out what you were thinking was the minute that you lost your advantage.

And you never knew when you might need an advantage. Even with your friends.

"Well," Emmett said, "I reckon the bank woulda been a mite embarrassed if folks knew we just carted the damn thing out the front door."

Choc nodded. "I'd say so."

Pretty Boy actually seemed pretty impressed by Emmett's tale, and he told him so. "Never thought of doin' it that way, Emmett. Think you might be on to something."

"Ahead of my time."

Choc nodded, chuckling. "I can always count on you to surprise me, Emmett."

"I just figure if there's an easy way and a hard way, I know which way I'm a-going."

Choc nodded his head slowly. "I'm too far down the road to turn back, but I know what you mean."

They sat in silence for a moment. Emmett had never seen Choc so contemplative before, and he wasn't entirely sure it was a good thing. Charlie Floyd was one of those fellas who was probably better off not thinking too much, especially given his chosen occupation. Or at least given the manner in which he performed his work. If he thought about things too much, he might hesitate, and then he'd be a dead man for sure.

Why Choc went into the banks with guns blazing, Emmett never understood. It just seemed like too much work. Emmett wasn't afraid of hard work; he just didn't much care for *unnecessary* work.

To be honest, Emmett had always thought Choc would have been better off not robbing banks at all. He was just a little too volatile.

One minute he was calm and thoughtful, and the next he could kill a man with almost no thought at all.

Emmett had seen that anger flash in his direction once or twice, and the only thing that saved them both was his poker face. Choc just never knew for sure if he'd come out on top, and he wasn't quite crazy enough to find out.

No, Choc shouldn't have been a bank robber—even though he was good at it. Emmett figured a man with a temper like Choc's should have been a boxer or even a wrestler.

The name "Pretty Boy Floyd" even sounds like one of them wrestlers.

"What are you thinking about, Emmett?"

"I was thinking I wouldn't mind running across Bonnie Parker sometime," Emmett mused.

Choc just shook his head. "Don't even ponder it, Emmett. Woman's crazy as an outhouse rat."

Emmett chuckled. "S'pose she'd hafta be, running around like she does."

"On the other hand, people sure can make up a lot of bull."

"I know that."

Choc gave Emmett a look. "You ever gonna settle down?" he asked.

Emmett was a little surprised at the question. Choc was a friend, but the man had never really gotten into Emmett's personal business before. Which may have been how they'd stayed friends.

Emmett thought for a moment. "Don't know exactly what I want, Choc," he said. "But I know one thing."

"What's that?"

"She's gotta be something special."

Choc nodded.

"Figure I'll know her when I see her," Emmett said.

"Fair enough."

Emmett nodded, and Choc got up to leave. "Appreciate the help."

Emmett waved his hand. He'd never refused Choc a night's sleep or a jug whenever he was on the run, which seemed to be most of the time ever since that mess up in Kansas City.

"You know that sonuvabitch J. Edgar says he's gonna start executing bank robbers."

Emmett shrugged. "Good thing I'm not one."

Choc looked at him a moment. "How come you never asked me?"

"Asked you what?"

Choc laughed. They both knew he meant whether or not Choc had really killed Frank Nash. Emmett didn't figure he had, but he also figured the less he knew about it, the better. If the law asked you questions, sometimes it was better not to have any answers at all instead of having to make something up.

Emmett might have broken the law here and there, but he wasn't a fan of lying. He was a straight shooter, literally and figuratively.

But Emmett couldn't see himself answering any questions from any lawman when it came to Choc. Once you had your picture up in the post office and the FBI on your trail, that was all she wrote. So far, he'd never been asked a single question about Choc that he'd felt uncomfortable answering. Not by any lawman, anyway.

But the way things were going, he knew that day might come sooner than he thought. They both knew it. The funny thing was, Choc had told practically everyone he met that he'd had nothing to do with it. He'd even told that to the newspaper reporters who'd caught up with him from time to time. And Emmett thought he'd even called *them* himself to share that story once or twice.

That was one reason he didn't figure Choc had done it. Emmett had never known the man to disavow any of his deeds, good or bad.

But for some reason, he didn't seem to want to make the claim to Emmett unless he asked.

"Emmett?"

"Yeah?"

"So how come you never asked?"

Emmett thought for a moment, then said, "Guess it felt kinda . . . *disrespectful.* Figured you'd tell me if you wanted to, and if you didn't, well, that's all right, too."

Choc looked at him for a long time, as if he were considering whether to just come out and tell Emmett what happened. After a moment, he made his decision. "Don't believe everything you read in the papers," he said with finality in his tone.

"Hardly read 'em," Emmett said, and that was certainly true.

The next time Emmett heard anything about his friend Choc, it was on the radio. Reports were that Pretty Boy Floyd been shot and killed in an Ohio cornfield by the famous G-man Melvin Purvis, the same fella that had got Dillinger. Speaking of which, Choc had been public enemy number one ever since John Dillinger had been killed, so Emmett had known it was just a matter of time for Choc, even if he himself hadn't.

Nobody stayed at the top of the most wanted list for too long.

And that was really what made Emmett decide never again to rob a bank. He'd gotten away with an awful lot of money the one time he'd tried it, and he was surely tempted to do it again, but he sure didn't want to end up like Charlie Floyd, always on the run, always looking over his shoulder. It was funny that Choc had asked that night if he wanted to settle down, because Emmett had actually been thinking about that lately.

One day, he wanted to find a wife and have a family, to build something that would live on after he was gone. Emmett thought that was where true happiness was surely to be found. Little did he know it would take him another twenty-five years or so to start that family—but when he did, his wife and child would bring him every bit of happiness that he'd figured they would.

"Shoulda tried it your way, Emmett."

Emmett nodded. He thought for sure he'd come up with a better way than Choc and Dillinger and all the rest of them—namely, robbing the bank in such a way that nobody knew it at the time.

Going in at night was a lot better than having to shoot your way out and maybe killing somebody in the process, which now meant the death penalty if you were caught.

Later, Emmett realized that that conversation was really Choc's way of saying goodbye. It was the last time they ever spoke.

After the news had gone public, Boots wanted to go up to Sallisaw, Oklahoma, for Pretty Boy's funeral—and to rob the bank in town during the service, which was sure to be a spectacle and keep all the cops in town pretty busy—but Emmett refused.

Although he had to admit, his old friend probably would have appreciated the gesture.

As it turned out, the funeral was "everything a funeral ought not to be," as the papers called it, with literally tens of thousands of people from out of town creating havoc at the cemetery and the funeral home and everyplace else they spilled over into.

Emmett heard all about it on the radio.

He played poker the day of the funeral and won every pot, which he considered a proper tribute to his old friend, and when things died down a little, he and Chester drove up to Choc's hilltop gravesite in Akins, just west of the Arkansas border.

For some reason—he never really knew why—Emmett had kept one of the leather-bound folders he'd taken from the bank's safe down in Grandview, Texas. He hadn't even looked at it too closely before, figuring it was probably just gobbledygook like the rest of them.

But there, on Choc's grave, he opened it up and was happy to see that it was just as he thought—some poor soul's promise to pay their thieving bank an awful lot of money. Emmett didn't understand most of the writing, but he knew numbers, and this one said $2,725.00.

"Must be a palace!" Ches said.

"Must be."

Emmett took a kitchen match from his coat pocket, striking a flame between his thumb and forefinger. Though the early November day was cold and windy, somehow that last mortgage caught hold of the fire right away and drew it in like an old friend.

Ches laughed as the thing went up like a torch. Emmett held on to it as long as he could, and then he dropped it on Choc's grave. The onetime bank robber and his brother watched that last mortgage burn until it was only ashes, which then caught in the breeze and floated out across the cemetery.

"Ashes to ashes," Ches said, and Emmett nodded.

"Think he's watching us?" Ches whispered.

"Could be," Emmett answered.

"Think he's lookin' up or lookin' down?"

Emmett smiled. "Reckon that's not for man to judge."

CHAPTER 16

My bank robbin' days are over, Chester," Emmett told his brother on the way back to Cache. The violent end met by his old friend Choc had caused Emmett to do quite a bit of thinking lately. He'd taken stock of things and decided not to put his boots in those particular footsteps again. "I'm movin' on with my life."

Chester considered this for a moment. "That mean you're done with gambling and whiskey, too?"

Emmett just looked at him. "Didn't say I was crazy. Just movin' on."

The way Emmett saw things, he would have had to have been crazy to leave whiskey behind. There was just too much money to be made, and, like poker, he was just too good at making it. Emmett could no more stop bootlegging than leave a fat poker pot in the middle of a table full of gin rummy players.

In spite of Prohibition's end, Oklahoma was still as dry as a bone, and the good citizens of the state were just as thirsty as they ever were. The change in federal law didn't mean a whole lot when the sale of alcohol was still barred by the state constitution.

As a matter of fact, it had been the federal government that had insisted on that provision when the state was first admitted to the union, out of fear that white store owners on the reservations would try to keep the Indians drunk so they could cheat them out of money the government had given them for their land.

Emmett was of a mind that regardless of race, creed, or color, if a man—or a woman, for that matter—wanted to drink, it should be left up to them, and the government should just stay out of the whole deal. And since there were eager buyers for his liquor, he was more than willing to sell it, prohibition regulations or no.

Emmett's motto was live and let live, and bootlegging was a mighty good living.

While it never seemed fair to him that, after the Twenty-First Amendment was passed, a fella could cross the border into Missouri and buy whiskey nice and legal while it was still against the law in Oklahoma, Emmett was perfectly willing to take advantage of that particular inconsistency between state and federal law.

Oklahoma was OK by him!

Another inconsistency in his business arose around that time, although he saw it as more of a "good news / bad news" type of situation. The good news was that there wasn't an army of federal agents beating the bushes for bootleggers. The bad news was the same, because most of those federal agents could be bribed, which generally meant fairly decent protection for his business.

Once the federal boys took a powder, Emmett had to worry about a revolving door of various county sheriffs and their deputies, which meant he could be looking over his shoulder at a brand-new face or two every time there was another election. You didn't just walk up to the new sheriff in town and hand him a bag of money and a jug to look the other way, because half the time, that was the very reason the voters had swept the other fella out of office.

That was one good thing about the federal agents. They seemed to stick around awhile, and the longer they did, the better Emmett got to know them. The only thing some of those fellas loved more than bribe money was drinking up the very thing they'd sworn to confiscate.

Emmett kept a low profile for a while, moving his still deeper in the woods and depending on his loyal crew to take care of business, which he did by paying them well and returning their loyalty in kind. It didn't hurt that, as noted before, nobody of right mind ever crossed Emmett Long.

But even Emmett knew he needed to start finding some legal ways to make money, too, if for no other reason than that he didn't trust the government. For all he knew, if the right (or wrong) politicians took office, they could legalize whiskey and even mandate its sale in every dime store in the state.

You just couldn't depend on the government for any sense or consistency at all sometimes.

Emmett began to use his hard-earned but ill-gotten gains to buy and lease land all around Cache and beyond.

There were a lot of Comanche in the area who owned leases on government land that they weren't using, so Emmett would give them a fair price and take over the lease for them. Sometimes he'd buy the land outright. They all knew and trusted Emmett already as a fair dealer from when he'd employed old Big Talker as a scout against the federal agents as well as, of course, from when Emmett would buy their votes for a dollar a piece to elect the "right" sheriff, which he continued to do on occasion.

He started buying up cattle, too, since he had all that land for grazing, and that was the beginning of his transition from bootlegger to rancher. Breeding and raising cattle was hard work, but Emmett enjoyed it because he was still his own boss. If anyone had told him when he'd left home as a boy that he'd be back working the land one day, Emmett would have laughed in his face. He hated sharecropping more than anything.

But working land you owned put a whole other face on it. It felt different somehow. All those years, Emmett had thought he hated hard work, but he really just hated working hard for somebody else.

As a rancher, Emmett noticed a difference in the way folks treated him, too. He had always been known as a fair-minded and tough man, but a man who lived on the wrong side of the law nonetheless. A man you didn't cross. A man who was respected but also feared.

Now he was becoming known as a legitimate businessman, and newfound respect was paid him by local ranchers and cowboys. Emmett was approaching thirty years old, and he felt like things were starting to go pretty well in his life.

That's not to say, however, that he'd sown his last wild oats.

Emmett played in a regular Friday night card game at the Altus Hotel, which was located about forty miles due west from Cache in Altus, Oklahoma.

Altus was a town of about eight thousand at the time, which made it at least ten times bigger than Cache, and that meant that the poker was a little more exciting for Emmett, for two reasons. One—everybody in and around Cache knew Emmett's poker skills and would never gamble with any serious money. And two—Emmett had more money than anyone in Cache anyway. Half the fun of poker was bringing a rich fella down a peg or two—unless you were the rich fella.

So occasionally a big spender with money and no knowledge of Emmett's skill would wander into Altus, and Emmett would send him packing with considerably less folding money in his wallet.

Sometimes they even lost the wallet.

Emmett almost always won, and he didn't even cheat to do so, but the real reason he never missed a game in Altus was because he'd run into a dark-haired, earthy chambermaid by the name of Lola, who'd stopped by Emmett's room one Friday afternoon after he'd requested fresh towels and hadn't left until Saturday morning.

That was the only Friday night game Emmett missed that entire summer.

Lola's husband, Max, worked the hotel desk in the evenings and had even introduced Emmett to his comely wife, never noticing how she noticed the tall, handsome cowboy from Cache.

Emmett, however, noticed her notice.

Max received a cut of each game in exchange for keeping the table full and the law blind—although the latter probably wasn't necessary, since the Jackson County sheriff's cousin sat in most weeks.

After Emmett noticed Lola notice him, he started arriving early and booking a room in order to "rest up" for the game that evening—or so he told her husband, who was only too happy to book another room for the hotel's owners, since he also collected a bonus when they reached full occupancy.

Each time Emmett checked in, after he'd paid in cash and signed the register, Max would say, "Rest up, Emmett!" in that irritating, singsong voice of his, and Emmett would give him a nod, go upstairs, and cuckold the clueless clerk.

Several times, if the game happened to start late.

Which it often did, if that was what Lola wanted. Because Lola usually got what she wanted, just like in the song that would be written nearly twenty years later.

This arrangement worked out well for everyone concerned, until the last Friday in August, which was a sticky summer night without a breeze or a cloud in the sky.

Emmett realized later that it must've been exactly nine thirty when the door to his room crashed open, because Lola had brought in some crazy cuckoo clock that night and hung it above the bed. He'd seen her set it exactly thirty minutes behind the actual time, probably to get a little extra cuckolding out of him before the game started at ten.

Not that Emmett minded. Again, whatever Lola wanted, Lola could have.

None of which mattered to Emmett when the dark silhouette burst in on the first cuckoo and stood in the doorway with only the glint of a .38 reflecting off the dim bulb from the hallway.

The room was quiet in spite of the violent entry, and Emmett knew immediately that the backlit figure had to be Max, because Lola hadn't screamed or even let out a peep.

Either that or Lola had another boyfriend besides himself.

Emmett wasted no time, regardless of who it was. He was out of bed with his pants up before the cuckoo reached five.

He faced the silhouette.

"Think you'd best—"

He never finished the sentence, because Max raised the gun and fired five shots into his stomach before Emmett could make it to the doorway and take his gun away, which scared Max so badly that he turned and ran from the room, down the stairs, and supposedly never stopped until he got to California.

Emmett turned and shot the clock, and that was when Lola started screaming.

He ignored her and grabbed his shirt, putting it on out of habit more than anything else as he stumbled out of the room. He managed to get down the stairs without collapsing, but it was difficult. Emmett felt like his guts were on fire and he was trying for all the world to hold them inside.

He staggered outside the hotel, where several horrified guests who'd heard the shots had gathered. In the silvery moonlight, he looked quite ghoulish, the front of his shirt covered in blood that looked black and shiny, almost like oil.

He reached for a heavyset man in a dressing gown, who stared at Emmett in horror as he grabbed a handful of nightshirt. "Doctor," Emmett gasped.

"Uh . . . six blocks down. White picket fence."

Emmett let go of the man's shirt and lurched in that direction.

"Knock loud, he's hard of hearing!" the man added helpfully.

By the time Emmett got to the doctor's house, which was indeed adorned by a white picket fence, he'd lost quite a bit of blood. He pounded on the door since he couldn't speak. After what seemed like hours, the porch light came on, and an elderly man in a robe opened the door.

The doctor took one look at Emmett and pulled him inside, at which point he nearly collapsed onto an examination table in the parlor. The doctor opened Emmett's shirt and was stunned to see his bullet-ridden torso.

Just then Chester rushed in. It was the first time he'd made the trip from Cache for poker night at the Altus Hotel, and it would most certainly be the last. "What happened, Emmett?"

"You know this man?" the doctor asked.

"That's my brother!"

"Well, help me get him up on the table!" the doctor ordered.

They lifted Emmett onto the gurney. The doctor cut away Emmett's shirt as Ches took off his boots, which were full of blood. The doctor quickly washed his hands and then stood over Emmett, who appeared to have fallen unconscious.

"What are you waitin' for, Doc?" Chas said. "Do something!"

The doctor turned to Ches and shook his head. "There's nothing I can do."

Just then Emmett sat up and grabbed the doctor by his collar, turning the old man around to face him. It was obvious that it took an extraordinary effort to do so. He spat blood out onto the floor and pulled the doctor's face to an inch from his own. "What you can do . . . is stitch me up. Understood?"

The doctor, who looked like he'd seen a ghost, could only nod his head.

"Good," Emmett said and lay back down on the table.

"Go get some ice," the doctor barked to Chester, who nodded and started toward the door. He stopped and turned around. "Where?"

"The hotel!"

"The hotel," Chester repeated. "Gotcha." He started out again, but then he stopped in the doorway. "How much?"

"As much as you can find!" the doctor screamed. "And then get some more!"

Chester charged out the door as the doctor and his wife worked on Emmett, who had mercifully passed out as the doctor probed and pulled at his wounds, desperately trying to remove the bullets. After three hours, he'd gotten all but two—both of which ultimately were to remain in Emmett's body for the rest of his life.

"Go next door, and wake up Jimmy at the funeral home!" the doctor barked at Chester.

"No, Doc!"

"Tell him I need a coffin!" he yelled. "A cheap one!"

Chester did as he was told, thinking Emmett was no more.

Inside the house, the doctor finally stopped the bleeding, stitched up Emmett's wounds, and gave him an extra sedative. Then he collapsed in a chair beside the gurney and called for Chester, who came back inside.

"I've done my best," the doctor said, exhausted. "We need to get him down to St. Jo's."

Chester looked from Emmett to the doctor, confused. "He's alive?"

"Of course he's alive, you damn fool! I'm not sending a dead man all the way down to Houston!"

"Praise the Lord!" Chester shouted.

"Where's that ice you fetched?"

Just then, the mortician and his son carried in a pine box. Chester looked at it in dismay. "Ain't ya got one a' them cherry-wood deals?"

They ignored Chester and lined the coffin with blankets before placing Emmett inside, after which they poured ice over his body. Then they carefully loaded the coffin into the back of the hearse.

Just before they closed the door, Ches told the driver, "Don't you put that lid on, now!"

Emmett spent several weeks in one of the best hospitals in Texas. He lost four pints of blood, several feet of intestines, and one cuckoo mistress, but he made it back home to Cache alive and well. He never heard from Lola again, but Ches said he heard she'd run off with a Fuller Brush man.

"What's a Fuller Brush man?" Emmett answered.

Lola's husband, Max, came back to Comanche County several years later, only to be shot and killed in an alley behind a grocery store about a week after his return.

Chester couldn't help himself. He had to ask Emmett if he knew anything about it.

"Nope," Emmett answered. "I don't hold grudges. That whole business was just me being in the wrong place at the wrong time with the wrong person."

Ches thought on it. "Think that's what happened to Max?"

Emmett shrugged. "Wouldn't be at all surprised."

CHAPTER 17

Emmett met the first woman he'd ever wanted to marry when he was handing out dollar bills for votes to reelect the sheriff of Comanche County. He liked this fella pretty well, as he didn't seem to be all that interested in nosing around out in the woods, which meant that Emmett could keep his still in one place for longer periods of time. His moonshine was selling real well, and he wasn't doing too badly with his legitimate businesses, either.

Truth be told, he probably didn't need to pay any of the locals to vote anymore, but it had become something of a habit.

Now, when the Comanche heard he'd be around with fresh lettuce, they'd all just stop by to grab a quick buck at Big Talker's place, which was where Emmett first saw her. The last of the locals had gone, and it was just him and Big Talker chewing the fat when the wild woman appeared.

She was dark and shapely, with long black hair pulled back into a single braid. It was obvious she was Native, although it seemed to

Emmett she probably had a white parent or grandparent as well. She had an Indian teenager by the ear and was practically dragging the poor kid across Big Talker's dirt yard toward the house.

Emmett stood up when they banged through the screen door, but Big Talker remained seated in his big overstuffed chair, unimpressed by the commotion.

It generally took a lot to impress Big Talker, which was another reason Emmett liked talking to him. He always got the straight dope with no embellishment, unless, of course, it was concerning one of his "visions." Then all bets were off.

The woman pushed the kid into the center of the room. "You better tell this son of a bitch to shape up!"

The kid pulled away—or rather, the angry woman released him—and straightened his collar. "She's crazy, Dad! I didn't do nothing!"

"The hell you didn't," the woman said, and then turned to Big Talker. "They was gambling again, Mister Saupitty. Took my brother for six dollars!"

Emmett's ears perked up. He might just like this kid.

"What are *you* smiling about, mister?" the woman demanded, her black eyes flashing Emmett's way.

"Emmett Long, ma'am," Emmett said, tipping his hat. The woman's eyes opened wide and then narrowed, as if she suspected a ruse, but Emmett just smiled and finally she turned to Big Talker, who nodded.

The woman softened. "I heard of you."

"Anything good?" Emmett asked.

"I think my brother may have took a little of your whiskey once."

"Took?" Emmett raised an eyebrow.

She looked as if she regretted her admission. "That's how he said it."

"He still around?" Big Talker asked.

"Of course," she said, looking a little scared.

"Must've paid, then," Big Talker said, chuckling. "Or else it was just a taste."

The woman shrugged. "He said you was nice about it."

Emmett laughed. "Guess it was just once."

The woman finally smiled. "Yeah, I think so."

Big Talker laughed again. "Nobody 'takes' twice."

"Didn't catch your name," Emmett said, causing the woman to blush. It was clear she was warming up to the tall cowboy.

"Ruby," she said. "Ruby Bluewater."

"How 'do, Ruby."

Big Talker finally stood up, walking over to the kid Ruby had just dragged into the house by his ear. "Emmett, this is my son, Larry."

The boy stuck out his hand, and Emmett shook it. "The one at Fort Sill?"

Larry nodded. Emmett meant the Fort Sill Indian School.

"Thought your hair was a little short."

Larry grinned. "They cut it off soon's I got there."

"Don't bother you none?"

Larry shrugged. "It'll grow back."

Emmett smiled and looked over at Big Talker. "Got a good head on his shoulders." He glanced at Ruby. "If he can keep it there."

Larry laughed, and Ruby flashed her temper again. "He stole from my brother, mister," she said.

"Your brother drew to an inside straight!" Larry replied.

Emmett laughed. "You like cards?"

"If there's a chump around."

Ruby took a swing at Larry, but Emmett caught her arm before she made contact. She looked like she was about to take a swing at

Emmett, too, but only for an instant. The look in his eye calmed her down pretty quick.

Emmett released her carefully and took a step back, as if he'd just set a spring trap and wanted to steer clear in case it snapped back. He took out his wallet, removing six one-dollar bills. "Larry, how 'bout I give Ruby here six dollars for her brother, and you find a new . . . partner."

Larry looked a little sad about losing what was apparently a terrible poker-playing buddy, but then he looked at Ruby and rubbed his ear, nodding. "OK."

Emmett handed the money to Ruby, who looked almost as dissatisfied as Larry.

"He better not take any more of my brother's money."

"I beat him fair and square," Larry protested, but Big Talker stood up to separate the two.

"I'll talk to him, Ruby," the old man said. "Emmett?"

Emmett looked at Big Talker and then got the hint. He opened the door and waited. Ruby softened again and smiled. "Thanks, Mister Saupitty." Emmett ushered her outside as Big Talker smiled from ear to ear. He'd obviously seen how Emmett had been looking at Ruby.

Once they were outside, Big Talker gave Larry a playful slap upside the back of his head. "How much you really get?"

Larry smiled slyly and pulled out a wad of bills.

Outside, Emmett chatted with Ruby. She worked in the laundry at the boarding school, where her little brother and his friend Larry were students.

"You don't approve of gambling?" Emmett asked. He found Ruby attractive, aside from her cussing, that is. He didn't care much for that, although he could live with it. But intolerance for poker would be a deal breaker.

"I love gambling," Ruby answered. "I just don't like to lose."

Emmett smiled.

Once he'd sent Ruby on her way, he went back inside to say good-bye to Big Talker. He and Larry were counting out the wad of bills, separating the ones, fives, and tens.

Emmett let out a low whistle. "That all from the school?"

"Some of it's from billiards in Lawton," Larry said. "We go on weekends sometimes."

"Billiards, huh?" Emmett asked, looking at the piles of cash.

A month later, Emmett had taken Ruby off the school's payroll and moved her into his house in Cache, where he also lived with his parents, John and Etta Long. It was a big house, and they all got along reasonably well, although Ruby could be a bit of a wild card. She had a temper, as she'd demonstrated at their first meeting, but she managed to behave around Emmett's parents. He idolized his mother in particular and would countenance no disrespect for her from anyone, even if he were falling in love with her.

He also asked Big Talker's son, Larry, to introduce him to his friends down at the pool hall, which was where Emmett ran into a young man by the name of Rick Burwell. Rick was a ne'er-do-well and a drifter about ten or twelve years younger than Emmett, who would normally not have found him to be very good company, except for the fact that Rick was an exceptionally good pool player and an even better con man.

Emmett and Boots had known Rick for a few years, but they hadn't seen him around lately, and neither of them had ever shot pool with him.

Rick was originally from Brownsville, Texas, but now he traveled from town to town, hustling pool. He'd make his way down to Brownsville and then back up to Oklahoma and Missouri, stopping along the way wherever he wasn't known to beat the local yokels out of their hard-earned money.

Emmett was pretty sure his old buddy Choc had run him out of Kansas City, and even though Choc was gone now, he didn't think Rick would be going that far north without protection, which was what gave Emmett the idea to stakehorse him.

All forms of gambling interested Emmett, but he was especially fond of games with odds that could be improved in interesting ways.

Rick's acting talent, combined with his skill with a cue stick, improved the odds considerably at the pool halls between Dallas and St. Louis for the next several months. Emmett, Boots, and Rick went out on the road to see what they could make, and they made a considerable amount.

Rick would go in first, get in a game, and show some level of skill, but not too much, in order to set up the suckers. Boots would work the crowd for bets once the money game was set, and Emmett would hang back and observe, watching the crowd for whoever might be trouble if things got a little rowdy.

Which they inevitably did.

The difference between card sharks and pool hustlers was usually the muscle. Men who frequented high-stakes poker games typically settled up with no problem, although there was the occasional exception, of course. But in a pool hall, it seemed like the men who lost their money were almost always eager to fight about the outcome. Emmett figured it was because poker players could never be sure if the other guy had cheated or was just lucky, but if you're hustled at pool, it's pretty obvious to the entire room.

"Not sure it's the money so much as the embarrassment of losin' it in front of all their friends," Emmett would say, and Boots would have to agree.

By the end of the final game, there would usually be a few hundred dollars in Boots's boots and more than a few angry men with cue sticks in their hands looking to prevent his exit.

By the end of the night, Boots and Rick would be hiding under the pool table while Emmett, who was six foot one and 215 pounds of mean muscle, took care of all those men with cue sticks.

Emmett cleaned up more pool halls than a regiment of janitors, and the three of them cleaned up in other ways, too, splitting thousands of dollars over the course of their trip.

It wasn't until they got back to Cache that Emmett finally decided to deal with Rick, who'd been taking more than his share of the winnings. The young hustler obviously thought his acting skills were a little bit better than they actually were.

Emmett wasn't quite as gullible as Boots, who'd never noticed the side bets Rick had been making. What irritated Emmett the most was that he'd been more than fair with Rick, splitting the pot three ways even though the stakehorse usually got the largest cut. And on top of that, Emmett was the one who had to fight every night.

Boots couldn't believe it. "How dumb can he be?"

But Rick wasn't so dumb after all, because when Emmett and Boots showed up at the rooming house, his landlady said he'd just lit out.

Owing three months' rent.

Emmett chalked it up to a lesson learned, figuring Rick was long gone, but the next day, when he rode his horse into town, there was Rick coming out of the hardware store with what looked like camping supplies. Once he saw Emmett riding toward him like one of the Four Horsemen of the Apocalypse, he dropped his things and ran across the street and straight into the bank, where he figured he'd be safe.

He figured wrong.

Emmett rode right through the double doors of the bank and lassoed Rick, catching him next to the assistant manager's desk. He tightened the rope and pulled him outside by the ankles, all the way down the front steps and right out into the middle of the street, where Rick willingly turned over every dollar he'd stolen and quite a few more.

He was shaking like a leaf, and a crowd had gathered, so Emmett let him go without another word, riding off into the sunset with a full wallet and a story for Boots.

Part of the story being that Emmett later owned that particular bank.

Boots liked the story, but he liked his cut even better.

Nothing like a three-way split with only two partners.

Not long after that, Emmett came home early one day and heard Ruby call his mother a name—a name he'd always sworn no man would ever get away with calling his sweet mother.

Ruby was lucky she wasn't a man.

Emmett walked into the kitchen, where his mother and Ruby were arguing across the table. They stopped and looked at Emmett.

He had a lasso in his hand.

Ruby, like everyone else in town, had heard about what happened at the bank a few days before.

She left without another word, and Emmett never saw her again.

He never saw Rick again, either, although you might say their paths would cross indirectly many years later.

And the kid who'd brought them all together graduated from the Fort Sill Indian School a couple of years later, landed at Utah Beach on D-Day with Brigadier General Theodore Roosevelt Jr., and sent the very first Comanche coded combat message, which was "*Tsaaktʉ nʉnnuwee. Atahtu nʉnnuwee.*"

Which meant, "We made a good landing. We landed in the wrong place."

Kind of like Ruby and Rick.

But because of how he'd dealt with those two, Emmett would soon meet the second woman he ever wanted to marry, and she would change everything.

Emmett finally landed in the right place.

CHAPTER 18

As the 1930s came to a close, Emmett's bootlegging operation was running smoothly, with very little interference from law enforcement. Even after the ratification of the Twenty-First Amendment, Oklahoma wouldn't repeal its own state prohibition laws for many years, which meant the federal authorities were out of the picture. And without the feds looking over his shoulder, the local sheriff's zeal for temperance was often tempered by his own taste for whiskey and, in Comanche County, at least, his taste for Emmett's bribe money.

Fortunately for Emmett, the current sheriff responsible for law and order in Cache and the surrounding area had an appetite for both. Emmett kept him in whiskey and a little spending money, and he added a few dozen votes come election time. Everybody was happy, including Emmett's customers, who swore his whiskey was the best in the state.

Things were so easy that Emmett even brought his still in from the woods and into town, facilitated by a friendly mortician with a fondness for drink and a nice patch of land behind his funeral home.

The locals told more than a few jokes about stopping by for a stiff one, of course.

Emmett's land holdings increased, as did the size of his herd, but in spite of his business success, he remained a restless soul. There were always women interested in the company of a handsome and prosperous cowboy, but none of them held his interest for very long.

He built beautiful rodeo grounds in Cache, promoting some of the best events in the county and riding broncs and bulls for excitement. But when a particularly fierce bull named Six threw him off and broke Emmett's leg, that put an end to his rodeo days.

Emmett had just turned forty years old.

They called that bull Six because six seconds was the longest anyone had ever lasted on his back, but the night Emmett broke his leg, he lasted seven.

As a reward for the mighty beast who'd bested him, Emmett put Six out to stud on his ranch, where the prize bull helped grow his herd, but like Emmett, old Six was still restless, and he made a habit of breaking through the fence to mount a neighboring rancher's cows in addition to his own.

The rancher, a hothead fairly new to the area, managed to catch old Six in the act and castrated the bull before herding him back through the fence.

When Emmett saw what the rancher had done, he stormed out to where two ranch hands were repairing the broken fence and told them to tell their boss that if he ever touched one of his cattle again, Six wouldn't be the only animal running around without his balls.

Fortunately for the rancher, he made a few inquiries around town, and his instinct for self-preservation managed to outweigh the demands of his short temper. He never crossed Emmett again.

Unfortunately for Six, he was renamed Four and spent the rest of his days watching another bull have all the fun.

As for Emmett, he was beginning to think he might never find the right woman with whom to share the spoils of his growing empire.

Until he met a diminutive schoolteacher with long chestnut hair and cornflower-blue eyes who stole his heart, along with the heart of every other cowboy who laid eyes on her one Friday night at the rodeo.

But Emmett almost missed the show.

"C'mon, Emmett. Geneva's friend's neighbor broke his foot. You can take his spot."

Emmett raised an eyebrow at his cousin G. W., whose fiancée was a pretty young thing named Geneva who just loved going to the rodeo. G. W. knew all about Six and Emmett's broken leg, but he was still trying to get Emmett back on one of those bulls.

"Everybody still talks about that time you roped some fella up in the second floor of the bank and drug him downstairs and up Main Street in his birthday suit."

Emmett ignored the extra relish G. W. put on that particular hot dog. He was used to hearing exaggerated versions of his exploits. "I'm headin' down to Dallas with a few barrels," he said. "Won't be back till Sunday."

Now it was G. W.'s turn to raise an eyebrow. "What good does it do to work like a dog if you never hang your head out the window to enjoy the breeze?"

Emmett was unconvinced, and he loaded up his truck that Friday afternoon for the delivery.

It was old Four, formerly Six, who changed Emmett's plans—and, by doing so, his entire life.

Emmett got a phone call from his hotheaded neighbor, who was no longer hotheaded or even his neighbor any longer. He'd sold off the parcel of land that bordered Emmett's ranch after the Great Castration just so there would be no possibility of any future misunderstandings that could invite the wrath of Emmett Long upon his head.

Good fences might make good neighbors, but distance makes the heart grow fonder.

"I don't know if you remember me, Mister Long—"

"I remember you," Emmett said gruffly.

"Well, sir, I don't want anybody to be confused—"

"Confused about what?"

"And I don't want nobody to get mad—"

"Mad about what?"

"It's kinda hard to say—"

"If you don't spit something out pretty quick, I'm gonna be confused *and* mad," Emmett said impatiently.

"Your bull's dead," said the rancher.

Emmett hung up the phone before the man could say another word.

When he arrived at the rancher's house, the bull formerly known as Six was in the back of the rancher's flatbed truck, and poor old Four was indeed as dead as a doornail.

"I swear I don't know how it happened, Mister Long," the rancher pleaded. "Found him just like that, right on my doorstep, almost like he was asking for my help."

Emmett looked at the quivering man with a mixture of pity and scorn.

"And you know I'm always ready to help a neighbor, Mister Long."

Emmett just shook his head and turned back to old Four. He noticed the rancher's hired help standing nearby, close enough to rush to their employer's aid in an emergency but far enough away that they could easily avoid any serious bloodshed. *Just as cowardly as their boss,* he thought.

Emmett knew immediately that the cause of death was natural. There were no signs of trauma, and the last time a vet had examined Six, shortly after he became Four, the doctor had noticed signs of a congenital heart defect. The treatment, had it not already been performed, was castration to eliminate rambunctiousness and retirement from the rodeo.

Emmett never told the rancher, of course. The man had purposely damaged his property, and he thought it better the man remain too scared to ever even think about something like that again.

Unlike the rancher, though, Four apparently had one more act of rebellion in him, and he had broken through *two* fences for old times' sake and then suffered a fatal heart attack afterward, *practically on the rancher's doorstep*, just as described. But to Emmett, it likely wasn't assistance the poor creature was looking for but revenge.

And it looked like the old bull had been willing to give his life in its pursuit.

Without a word, Emmett walked over to the rancher and held out his hand. The man dropped the keys to his truck into Emmett's palm. Emmett climbed in the vehicle and drove his bull back home, followed by one of the ranch hands in his own truck.

By the time Emmett was done with the business of bull retrieval, he was no longer interested in driving down to Dallas, and so he delegated that job to Chester.

And that was how a frightened rancher and a vengeful bull teamed up to introduce Emmett to the love of his life.

Eventually.

With a little help from Cousin G. W. and his fiancée.

Emmett decided that since his weekend was now free, he might as well go down to the rodeo.

"You change your mind about that bull?" G. W. asked when he saw Emmett walk up to where they were sitting.

"Not the one you're thinkin' of."

He exchanged pleasantries with Geneva, who mentioned something about her sister, but Emmett's mind had already moved on to other things—specifically, a beautiful girl down in the front row who seemed mesmerized by a fearsome horse one of the barrel racers had obviously ridden over to impress her. He watched as the girl instantly found the stallion's sweet spot between the shoulder blades and scratched, ignoring the cowboy on its back and immediately relaxing the beast.

That's a girl who knows how to handle dangerous creatures, Emmett thought.

The way she cast a spell over that horse reminded Emmett of that lady with the long blonde hair who'd ridden a white horse through the middle of some town without a stitch of clothes on.

"That's her, Emmett," Geneva said.

Emmett turned back to his cousin's future wife. "'Her' who?"

Geneva laughed, and even G. W. chuckled. "That girl you're staring at like she was a plate of fried chicken and you was starving," she answered. "That's my sister."

Geneva's sister was just about the prettiest girl Emmett had ever seen.

"What's her name?" Emmett asked without taking his eyes off her.

Geneva laughed again, trading a look with G. W. "Merl," she said.

"Merl," Emmett repeated, almost like a prayer. He turned to G. W. "I'll take that spot," he said.

"What spot?"

"Bull riding's next, ain't it?"

G. W. allowed that it was and looked at Geneva, who just laughed. Emmett wasn't like most men, but in one way, he was like all men. He'd just seen a pretty girl, and he wanted to impress her. And that was how Emmett climbed onto the back of a bull at the age of forty, after he'd promised his doctor he'd never again do so. He did it against his better judgment but in the spirit of Four, and also for the oldest reason on earth for which a man does almost anything.

He did it to impress a pretty girl.

He did it for love.

The last thing he saw as he climbed onto the back of a bull he had no business riding was that same pretty girl, with long brown hair spilling out from under her cowboy hat, getting into a truck on the other side of the arena as a man held her door. And Emmett knew he'd made a mistake.

He lasted all of two seconds on that bull.

"What happened, Emmett?" G. W. asked.

"Don't know," Emmett answered, but that was a lie.

"His heart wasn't in it," Geneva said, looking at Emmett. They both knew that she spoke the truth. Emmett's heart wasn't in his ride because it had been stolen, and they both knew who the guilty party was. "But I know where it got to," she said.

"I don't know what you two are talking about, but that was about the worst ride I've ever seen in my life," G. W. said. "Cain't you do better'n that, Emmett?"

"He'll do a lot better," Geneva said. "Just wait till the wedding."

G. W.'s eyes widened. "You getting married, Emmett?"

Geneva punched her fiancé's arm. "*We're* getting married!" She smiled at Emmett. "And my sister'll be there."

Merl came to her sister's wedding with a date, but Emmett didn't care. He thought she was the most beautiful woman he'd ever laid eyes on, and he was bound and determined to see as much of her as he possibly could. Merl remembered seeing him at the rodeo, and when he told her the story of Six-then-Four the bull, she laughed so hard she thought she'd split her sides. Her boyfriend practically had to drag her away from Emmett after the reception.

Emmett got in the habit of driving down to Bellevue, Texas, every chance he got to see her. Merl was a twenty-three-year-old schoolteacher who lived with her parents, and her boyfriend was the steady kind, although she always dropped everything and ran to Emmett's car as soon as he pulled up to the house.

On several occasions, she was sitting on the porch with her boyfriend, but she'd always hop in Emmett's car and go for a ride anyhow as soon as he appeared.

Her boyfriend was too scared of Emmett to challenge him directly, but whenever that happened, he'd take out his frustrations by storming to the woodpile behind her parents' house to chop firewood. Merl's father didn't particularly like what was happening, because Emmett was sixteen years older than his daughter, but his wife shushed him because they'd never had so much wood chopped as when Emmett came courting.

Sometimes they'd go for a drive, and sometimes they'd just sit in Emmett's car in front of her parents' house, talking for hours as they listened to her boyfriend chop wood. The two of them could talk for hours and never get tired, and neither one had ever met another person they found as endlessly entertaining.

Eventually, all else seemed to drift away, and it would be just the two of them in the car, in their own little world, as if no one and nothing else existed, talking and laughing late into the night.

Soon enough, Merl's boyfriend drifted away for real, and she and Emmett were married in a civil service ceremony, with no one present save for the justice of the peace and two witnesses they'd found at the courthouse.

When he got to the part about "love, honor, and obey," Merl was in such a hurry to be Missus Emmett Long that she blurted out "all of it" and caused one of the witnesses to bust out laughing.

The first time they ever kissed was when the justice of the peace told them to "go 'head," and Merl thought that was just about the most romantic thing she'd ever experienced.

At least until they checked into a Dallas hotel later that night.

When Merl's father found out what had happened, he drove straight to the Comanche County Sheriff's Office to see about getting his daughter back. He wasn't too much older than Emmett himself and thought maybe the sheriff would be sympathetic.

"Mister Owens," the sheriff said, "I can see you're upset."

"Upset?" Merl's father yelled. "'Course I'm upset! My daughter run off with that outlaw, and I want her back!"

The sheriff took hold of Mister Owens's elbow and gently guided him into the inner office, where he managed to calm him down enough to take a seat. "Mister Owens, your daughter obviously loves Emmett, if she run off with him."

"I don't care about that, she—"

"And I can tell you for a fact that he loves her, too."

"How do you know that?" Mister Owens demanded.

"Cause that's all Emmett talks about since they met," the sheriff said. "The whole town knows about it."

"The whole town?"

"Yes, sir. And there's something else the whole town knows."

"What's that?"

"If your daughter's married to Emmett Long, you won't ever have to worry about her again. Not for a minute."

"Is that so?"

"Yes, sir, it is."

Merl's father thought about that for a moment.

"Now, I bet your wife isn't near as upset as you."

"How'd you know that?"

The sheriff smiled. "Cause women know about matters of the heart. Don't they?"

Edd Owens shrugged. "Guess that's so."

"I know it's so," the sheriff said. "And what *I* know about is keeping people safe." He leaned in. "There ain't a safer place on earth for your little girl than as the wife of Emmett Long."

Mister Owens seemed to soften a bit.

"Now, why don't you go on home, and I'll bet when you get there, your daughter and her husband are gonna come around to see you and get everything all straightened out."

"I guess I could try that."

Merl's father stood up, and the sheriff walked him to the door. "You're gonna learn to appreciate your son-in-law, Mister Owens," he said. "Even love him, I'll bet."

The older man squinted at the sheriff. "How do you know that?"

The sheriff smiled. "Just got a feelin'," he answered.

And as it turned out, the sheriff was absolutely right.

CHAPTER 19

When Emmett and Merl came back from Wichita Falls as man and wife, they discovered that Emmett's house just outside of Cache had burned to the ground the night before. Emmett's mother, the only one home at the time, had been able to save just two things: the family Bible and her Singer sewing machine.

She was sitting beneath the cedar tree when they arrived, sewing machine in the grass beside her, the Bible open on her lap.

Emmett got out of the car and opened the door for his bride, ignoring the smoking shell of his former home. He brought Merl over to where his mother was reading the Good Book.

"Missus Long," Emmett said, "meet Missus Long."

His mother stood up and hugged her daughter-in-law, and the three of them talked for ten minutes before anyone bothered to mention the smoldering house less than a hundred feet away.

They all slept under the cedar tree that night.

The next morning, Emmett took Merl into town to show off his new bride. He introduced everyone he saw to the new Missus Long, an introduction that was met with great surprise around town. Minnie Simmons, who owned the Shamrock station, nearly passed out when Emmett introduced Merl as his wife. Emmett had been single for so long and was thought of as such an untamable man that no one thought he would ever actually settle down and get married.

"You must be a little wild yourself, honey," Minnie blurted out, causing Merl to blush furiously and Emmett to beam with pride. Before he could agree with Minnie's assessment, and Emmett *did* agree, Merl recovered and kissed Emmett right on the lips in front of both Minnie and her husband, Paul, who'd only just walked into the station with an old friend who was visiting from out of town.

"You may be right, Missus Simmons," Merl said, smiling sweetly, and Minnie nearly fainted again. Her husband, Paul, actually reached out and grabbed her elbow just in case. This would be one of Minnie's favorite stories to tell folks in town about the day Emmett showed up with a wife nobody ever expected to meet.

They got much the same reaction from others. Nobody could believe Emmett had gotten married, but they were all very impressed by the beautiful young woman who'd landed him.

Marriage suited them both. Everyone who knew him noticed a change in Emmett after he married Merl. There was just something about her that seemed to soothe his soul. She was the only person who could truly exorcise his inner demons, at least for many years, and Emmett's life was never the same after he found her.

To put it simply, Merl was Emmett's soul mate, and his soul mate brought him peace.

He was still a man to be feared, of course. A reputation like Emmett's wasn't created overnight, nor could it be erased so easily.

In many ways, Emmett was just as wild and stubborn as he had always been, even after their marriage. In spite of the fact that he was buying property, raising cattle, and acquiring thousands of acres in land leases—in other words, operating as a respectable business-man—Emmett was still a bootlegger and a gambler at heart, and he still greatly enjoyed those pursuits.

The difference was that once Merl came into his life, all of those things became secondary.

There was nothing Emmett wouldn't do for her.

Some thought that marriage had mellowed Emmett, but it was more like he'd just settled into a new life that he liked even better than the old one. And in that new life, there were new responsibilities and new ways to occupy his time.

Emmett was finally a happy man, and a happy man isn't ruled by anger.

Of course, Emmett had been able to control his temper before he met Merl; on the contrary, he'd always been a strong man with a great deal of control over himself and his emotions. But he'd also been known to let loose when he deemed it necessary, which was the dark side of such power.

After getting married, he just seemed to have fewer reasons to unleash his anger on others—probably as a result of both his hard-won and fearsome reputation and the contentment he'd found in married life.

As before, Emmett never went looking for trouble, but he didn't back down from it, either. But after Merl came into his life, trouble seemed to give him a wider berth, almost as if the universe sensed he was an even more formidable foe with her by his side. Merl was every bit his match, and Emmett loved her all the more for it.

Whether it was the wisdom that came with age, the happiness that came from Merl, or a combination of both, Emmett was now a satisfied man indeed.

There was only one thing that could have made their life together even happier.

A child.

They got to work on that almost immediately, and the day Merl told her husband she was going to have his baby, Emmett Long laid his head in her lap and cried.

No one except Merl saw the tears of joy in Emmett's eyes, but even if others had, they might not have believed it. Emmett Long hadn't cried since he was a child, and even back then, it was not a very common occurrence at all.

Emmett and Merl did all the typical things new parents do, from picking out names to fixing up a nursery in their home. Merl cooked for anyone who came to visit, and Emmett was always home in time for supper. It was the happiest time of their lives.

Oftentimes, they would sit out on the porch together for hours, just as they had when he was courting her. They might talk for a while, or they might just sit in silence and hold hands, but neither one of them ever tired of the other's company.

"Think it's a little girl," Emmett told her one evening as they sat looking up at the starry Oklahoma night.

She looked at him, a little surprised. "Think so?"

Emmett nodded. "Gonna be pretty, like her mama."

"Don't you want a little boy?" she asked, almost shyly.

Emmett shrugged. "Just want a little more a' you."

They talked for hours that night, about hopes and dreams and plans for their daughter. About their family, and children, and everything they both wanted.

"How many kids you want?" Emmett asked his wife.

"However many the good Lord wants us to have," she answered.

"I'll go for that."

On the night his daughter was stillborn, Emmett Long shed tears for the second time in his adult life. When he got the news that the baby had been strangled by her umbilical cord in her mother's womb, Emmett lay down on the floor of Merl's hospital room and wept unashamedly.

While Merl was sedated, Emmett cradled the tiny body of their daughter, Sandra Sue Long, refusing to let go of her until he gently placed her in the tiny casket at Cache Cemetery. When the lid was closed, Emmett wept again, blaming himself for the loss of their child. He truly believed what happened was God's punishment for all the wicked things he'd done in his life.

"I don't think I'm gonna be a father," he told his sister Carmen. "I done too many bad things."

Carmen shook her head. "God has a plan for all of us, Emmett," she said. "Trust in the Lord, and He shall provide."

Emmett wasn't so sure, but he supposed time would tell. When he brought Merl home from the hospital, they mourned the loss of their child together.

Not long after that, Merl's sister, Geneva, gave birth to a baby girl with a very serious heart defect. Emmett found a pediatric heart surgeon who was breaking new ground treating that specific disorder, and he took Merl, Geneva, G. W., and baby Jean to Philadelphia for the surgery, paying for everything out of his own pocket. There were five infants there for treatment; only two survived.

One was Geneva's child.

Having lost their own daughter, Emmett and Merl found comfort in the life of their niece.

But still they mourned and clung to each other even more tightly than before. And they prayed.

As it turned out, little Sandra brought them both closer to God, proving the truth of Carmen's words.

Neither of them ever gave up hope of having a family, and many years later, when Emmett was close to sixty years old, Merl got pregnant again. This time, the Lord had different plans, and their daughter, Mattie Lee Long, would fulfill Emmett's dream of fatherhood more than he ever expected.

Trust in the Lord, and He shall provide.

CHAPTER 20

The loss of his first child affected Emmett in ways nothing else ever had. Just as finding love later than most had expanded his heart, losing that baby seemed to break it in two.

As a man who'd spent his entire life mostly doing whatever he wanted to do whenever he wanted to do it, the first years of his marriage were filled with experiences he'd never expected. For the first time in his life, he understood what it was to love someone more than himself, and he also understood what it meant to lose someone like that, too. Some might have withdrawn into themselves after losing a child, but Emmett doted on Merl even more than he had before.

After losing a daughter and nearly losing a niece, Emmett began to see life in ways he never had before. He grew even closer to his wife, and she to him, and together, the two of them became almost as one.

Emmett had always been generous with friends and family, but with Merl's encouragement, he soon became quite a philanthropist in the community. They were particularly interested in helping the schoolchildren of Cache, as Merl had been a teacher in Texas before they were married, and she'd loved it. Most of the people in and around Cache were not well off financially, so the local schools were always in need.

Merl became friends with members of the school board and made it known that she and Emmett would like to help in any way they could. She thought that if the good Lord had decided they weren't going to be parents themselves, then helping out the children of the community was the next best thing.

And then little Mattie Lee was born.

Emmett was almost sixty years old when she was born, long after he figured he'd missed his chance to raise a family. Both he and Merl were caught completely off guard when she got pregnant, but it was the best surprise either of them could have hoped for. Merl was almost twenty years younger than Emmett, but she was still past the age when most women became new mothers, and they considered their new baby a gift from God.

"He works in mysterious ways, Emmett," Merl told her husband, and it was not long after that that Emmett invited Jesus into his heart. Emmett didn't entirely leave his old ways behind, but for the rest of his life, he mostly kept his temper in check, unless it involved insult to his wife or daughter.

And after the birth of his daughter, he became even more eager to support the local schools financially, since, to use a gambling analogy, he now had real skin in the game. His help didn't even need to go to the school Mattie was attending at the time. He figured just having a child in public school was a good enough reason to help out, and Merl agreed.

One evening, a teacher from the local high school stopped by to visit with Merl, dragging along her husband, who coached the basketball team. Emmett was taking a nap in the bedroom, Mattie asleep on his chest. When the coach happened to mention that the scoreboard in the gymnasium had stopped working right in the middle of a game, Merl excused herself and walked right into the bedroom.

"Emmett," she whispered. "Come in here, and listen to this."

Emmett gently laid Mattie back in her crib and went into the living room with Merl.

"Tell Emmett about that scoreboard," she said.

The husband repeated his story, and then it was Emmett who excused himself. The man, whose wife had apparently dragged him out of the house that night to go visiting, took that as his chance to stand up and suggest they say their goodnights.

"Hold on a minute, Coach," Emmett said, walking into the room holding a pillow over his shoulder like a knapsack.

Before the man could speak, Emmett swung the pillowcase over the dining room table and shook it, dumping its contents out for his startled guests to see.

There was no pillow in the case, but a huge pile of cash. Fives and tens, but mostly twenties, covering nearly the entire table.

"Get y'self a good 'un," Emmett said.

The man, slack jawed, managed to tear his eyes away from the cash and looked at Emmett. "A good what?"

"Scoreboard," Emmett answered. "This'll fix you up, won't it?"

The man looked back at the money, then back to Emmett. There must have been a thousand dollars in front of him. "I would think so!"

Emmett tossed him the pillowcase. "Come back if you need some more," he said. "Don't skimp."

After that, members of the school board made a habit of stopping by for a visit at Emmett's house whenever they needed something for the school, and Merl made sure she always had more pillowcases in the linen closet than she had pillows in the house, just in case.

At the end of each school year, any girl who needed a prom dress or any boy who needed a suit was sent to the Longs, and Merl would take care of things.

They were voted Parents of the Year for twenty-six years in a row, even after Mattie had graduated out of the public school system. The way Merl saw it, the good Lord had given them Mattie to ease the loss of Sandra, and all the other kids who came after that were reminders of their blessing.

By the time Mattie actually started elementary school, Emmett and Merl had already contributed tens of thousands of dollars to the high school that she wouldn't be attending for another eight or nine years.

Late in the summer of '66, Emmett got a call from one of his old outlaw buddies, Benny Binion. That was the year Emmett "temporarily unretired" from his life of crime so he could help Benny take the Las Vegas mob for half a million dollars using little more than their wits, quick-drying hair gel, and a pair of red-tinted aviator sunglasses that looked like something you might see Don Draper wearing on the television show *Mad Men*.

Emmett was reticent at first.

"I've got a kid now, Benny," he said.

"Got a few myself," Benny answered. "What's that got to do with the price of tea in China?"

Emmett smiled in spite of himself. Benny was always hard to resist when he had a scheme on his mind. "Not too much, I reckon."

"You got that right."

That night, after Mattie was asleep, Emmett took Merl out on the porch, and they sat awhile, looking up at the stars.

"Got a call today," Emmett said.

Merl waited.

"Benny," he continued.

After another pause, Merl said, "You go on."

"You sure?"

Merl smiled. She knew her husband had the itch, and if he'd spoken to Benny, that meant he was looking to scratch it. "We'll be fine," she said.

Emmett kissed her, and they went inside the house. The next morning, he kissed both of the women in his life, and then he flew to Las Vegas.

Any time Emmett got together with his pal Benny, the notorious gambler and casino owner, there was bound to be money and excitement—two things not even marriage and fatherhood could ever completely erase from Emmett's mind. Benny eventually went from bootlegger to mob boss to beloved Las Vegas icon over the course of his eighty-five years, but back then, he was still surrounded by a little madness, albeit with a method every step of the way.

He was Emmett's kind of guy.

Years later, he'd invite the whole Long family out to his casino in Vegas and let Mattie gamble with house money long before she was legally allowed to do so. She'd call him Uncle Benny and run around the world-famous Binion's Horseshoe casino having her way with those noisy, flashing slot machines, something Emmett never tired of watching.

But that was later. Back in the summer of '66, Caesars Palace was preparing for its grand opening, and Benny was persona non grata, which was why he needed Emmett to help him with his plan by walking out of the brand-spanking-new casino with a half million dollars in cash won at the high-stakes poker table with the help of that crazy hair gel.

Like they say, a little dab'll do ya!

The main thing Emmett and Benny had in common, besides a long criminal history and a deep love of gambling, was their charisma. When either one of them walked into a room, they kind of took it over. They both had a commanding presence no matter where they went, and they both used it to their advantage.

In the case of their Caesars Palace heist, it was Emmett who did all the commanding, since there was no way Benny could get away with cheating at cards anywhere in Las Vegas, because everybody knew him on sight. He was the king of Glitter Gulch, even though he'd only been out of Leavenworth for a few years after his conviction for tax evasion, staying for part of that time in the very same cell Emmett had called home back during the Great Depression.

Another thing they had in common.

Emmett checked into Caesars Palace right after the grand opening, just as Benny had suggested. They both figured that all the hoopla and festivities would also come with just enough confusion to make the joint ripe for a little mischief.

Other than the desk clerk and the bellboys, nobody paid much attention to the tall, quite respectable-looking man in the Western suit, complete with Stetson and well-buffed cowboy boots. He looked like what he had become, which was a well-to-do rancher. But he was also a man with a plan, and that plan included cheating the casino out of as much money as he possibly could.

Even without cheating, Emmett was still an expert card player. He hadn't lost his ability to count cards, read people, and prevent them from reading him. You can't cheat at poker successfully unless you can also win legitimately, and as he'd aged, Emmett's poker face had only become more inscrutable than it had been in his youth, and his capacity for patience had only increased.

But winning legitimately wouldn't have been nearly as much fun to Benny or Emmett, especially since the money they'd be helping themselves to would have otherwise lined the pockets of the Las Vegas mob.

Before he went down to play that first night, Emmett checked his "tools," namely that special hair gel that enabled him to mark the cards and a pair of aviator-style glasses that enabled him to see those marks.

It was just a matter of adding a chemical to the gel and a tint to the lenses, then adding poker skills to the mix.

Excited to be "back in the game," Emmett spent the first few hands getting a feel for the other players, as well as the dealer. *Who are the risk takers? Who pays attention, and who gets distracted? How often does the dealer change decks?*

It felt just like old times.

Once he got the rhythm of the game, it was time to go to work. For the first couple of hours, Emmett won enough to make things interesting, but not so much that the risk takers would drop out. It's the same story with most gambling strategies and the simple reason the house almost always wins in the end. The players keep playing because they want to win their money back.

In more ways than one, Emmett was just beating the casino at its own game.

Gradually, he picked up the pace, being careful not to give away his method of winning.

Once he'd racked up $25,000, Emmett went upstairs to get a good night's sleep. By then, he knew he was being watched pretty carefully by the floor managers as well as by the eyes in the sky, all of them trying to figure out if he was just a lucky old cowboy, a professional, or a cheat.

What they never figured out was that Emmett was all three!

He continued the same routine every day. He'd start playing around midnight, and by four, he'd cash in his chips and go upstairs to sleep. By the third day, the management of Caesars Palace was aware they were being hit by an old pro, and Emmett was being scrutinized as closely as anybody ever had. Even so, nobody could figure out how he was doing it—or even who he was. This was long before the days of credit cards and checked IDs, and just about anyone could check in and sign any name they wanted, as long as they had the cash to pay for their room.

After all, the casino wanted that cash. Who cared what your name was?

By day four, the casino manager added a couple of goons to the small army of employees now watching Emmett. He knew that Caesars would never let him walk out of there with a briefcase full of cash, or any luggage at all, for that matter. If he even looked a little heavier than when he arrived, they would search him.

But Emmett and Benny had thought of everything—and Emmett hadn't been stuffing cash in that briefcase just to leave it behind when he left.

Early on in his stay, Emmett had made friends with one of the restroom attendants on the main floor. He was an older black man, as many of the attendants were in those days, and Emmett tipped him well each and every time he was handed a towel. They were on a first-name basis by the second day, so when Emmett asked Jim to meet him at a coffee shop down the street after his shift was over, there was no hesitation.

Emmett bought him breakfast and laid out the favor he needed. "Need you to buy me a used car," he said. "Maybe a Caddy."

Jim, remembering the good tips, agreed to do so with no hesitation.

"Leave it for me in the parking lot. Don't use the valet."

Jim nodded. "No valet."

"Put the keys and directions to where it's parked in an envelope with my name on it, and leave it at the front desk."

"Is that it?"

"That's it."

"I can do that," Jim said. "But just one thing."

"What's that?"

"How do I pay for the Caddy?"

Emmett smiled and took out a wad of bills that could have choked Caesar's entire stable and peeled off $6,500. "Five for the car, fifteen hundred for you. How's that sound?"

Jim smiled and took the money. "Sounds pretty good to me."

They shook hands and went their separate ways. A couple of blocks away, Emmett went to his second meeting with another friend from the hotel. Jake was also a men's room attendant, and this time, Emmett bought lunch.

After a little small talk over sandwiches at the cafeteria, Emmett got down to business. "Tonight, while I'm playing poker, I want you to go to the front desk and pick up an envelope that was left for me. It has keys to a car and directions to where it's parked. Then go up to my room, take my suitcases down to the car, and put 'em in the trunk."

Jake nodded. He looked pretty interested, since Emmett had been tipping him very well, too.

"I'm gonna leave a map on top of the suitcases with directions to my place in Cache, Oklahoma. You drive the car there, and I'll give you $2,500."

"You'll be there?"

"If I'm not, you can keep the car." Emmett laughed. "But I'll be there, trust me."

"All right," Jake answered, and Emmett gave him enough money for gas and food and emergencies, with the promise of a whole lot more. Emmett had always been a good judge of character, and he had no doubt Jake would arrive as scheduled.

Emmett believed that you treated everyone with respect whether or not there was an immediate return. It was a belief instilled in him by his father, and it had almost always kept him in good stead.

That night, Emmett followed the same routine as he had for the past two weeks, except this time, he just broke even. The next morning, when he left his room, the goons followed him as usual, all the way down to the front desk. When he walked out the front doors with no luggage, the goons let him go. They probably thought he'd lost his nerve and just left the money behind.

They couldn't have been more wrong. Emmett had never lost his nerve a day in his life. He didn't have it on him just yet, but he'd walked out the door $500,000 richer, and Caesars never even learned his name.

It was the perfect heist. Emmett and Benny had beaten the house.

Boots picked him up at the Oklahoma City Airport and drove him to Cache, where the money arrived about when expected. Jake caught the bus back to Vegas a very happy man, and Emmett wired a quarter of a million dollars, less expenses, to another very happy man.

What happened in Vegas didn't *always* stay there, at least not when it came to Emmett and his old partner in crime, Benny Binion.

"Didja have fun, Daddy?" Mattie asked when he walked in the door.

Emmett kissed his wife and winked at his daughter. "Always do."

CHAPTER 21

After Emmett's big payday from Caesars Palace, he began looking around for other investment opportunities. Since he'd been expanding both his land holdings and his cattle-ranching business, he liked the idea G. W. came up with to take a look at Australia, which G. W. swore had plenty of both—and it was all quite cheap, as well. Nobody liked finding a good bargain more than Emmett did.

Chester used to say he wasn't sure what Emmett liked the best about horse trading, the horses or the trading, and there was a lot of truth to that. Emmett loved being a rancher and a cowboy, and he loved getting the better of whoever was buying or selling, no matter what was on the auction block.

When he finally saw the movie *Oklahoma!* several years after it was first released, he couldn't decide which character he liked better: the heroic cowboy or the snake-oil peddler who took such pleasure in swindling the townsfolk.

When Merl pointed out to her husband that the cowboy got the girl in the end, Emmett reckoned that it shouldn't be an either/or-type deal, but then he kissed her cheek and allowed that he wouldn't trade places with either one of them.

Which, of course, was exactly what she wanted to hear.

But she didn't quite know what to think when he next told her they would all be moving to Australia.

"Australia? What on earth for?"

"Lots of land and lots of cattle," Emmett replied but, upon noticing her furrowed brow, added that she shouldn't worry, since he and G. W. were going to fly over there and check things out before he sent for her and Mattie.

G. W., who was sitting next to his wife when Emmett said it, almost completely contained his surprise at the news of their trip, which was the first he'd heard of such a plan. And even as their husbands maintained their poker faces—for the most part—so did their wives, who knew their husbands all too well.

Merl looked at her sister, Geneva, and then back to Emmett. "Well, you boys have a good time."

Emmett quickly made arrangements, and the two of them headed Down Under on their scouting expedition.

Things did not go well.

First of all, almost as soon as they checked into their hotel, they discovered the local newspaper had printed a story about the wealthy cowboys who had just blown into town with a satchel full of cash looking to buy a cattle station in the area, which was what the Aussies called a ranch. Which basically meant the asking prices had all just gone up by 20 percent.

As an expert poker player used to holding his cards close until the most advantageous moment of revelation, Emmett was fit to be tied. The listing agent, who envisioned a nice, fat commission based on the purchase price, was quite a bit more enthusiastic about the story in the paper.

"I'd like it a whole lot better if you'd hold your tongue from here on out," Emmett told the man, who promised to do so. Emmett, who could spot a liar at fifty paces, was becoming less enthusiastic about finding a good deal. But he soldiered on, as the damage had already been done.

That afternoon, the agent took them for a drive across a cattle station of several thousand acres owned by a man he assured them had neither the time nor the inclination to care about what was written in the local newspapers. "He's a Lutheran," the agent said, as if that explained anything. Emmett just looked at G. W. as the man drove over a sandy berm and down toward what looked to be a shallow creek.

The creek turned out to be deeper than it looked, and the agent's Land Rover got stuck in the middle of the stream.

The agent looked at his watch, and then turned around to face his passengers in the back seat. "All right, then," he said and opened his door, wading out into the creek.

Emmett and G. W. followed suit, figuring the fellow was going to hike to the owner's house, which could be seen atop a nearby ridge.

To their surprise, the agent instead began to build a fire on the bank.

"We can hike it," Emmett said.

The agent looked up from the fire. "What's that?"

"Don't look too far off," Emmett said, referring to the ranch house. "No need for smoke signals."

The agent laughed and waded back into the water toward the disabled vehicle, removing an old leather suitcase from the rear compartment and bringing it ashore. Emmett and G. W. watched in silence as he opened the case and removed two small folding stools and a silver tea service.

"Tea time," he said cheerfully and took the pot down to the creek for fresh water to boil for tea. "Sit, please," he said, and Emmett and G. W. obediently sat on the stools while the agent pulled up a rock and prepared their midday refreshments.

The three men sipped their tea and talked about cattle station prices for a quarter hour, after which the three of them managed to push the Land Rover to a slightly shallower spot, where it started instantly, and they were once more on their way.

The owner of that particular station turned out to be none so ignorant of the news as the agent had predicted, and they left without an agreement as to what constituted a reasonable price.

Once back at the hotel, they ran into another American, this one a seller, and fell into a fortuitous conversation in the bar. Their new friend, Jack, had traveled to Australia to try to sell his station, although that was not at all the fortuitous aspect of the conversation.

"They kill you on taxes here," Jack said, downing a shot of whiskey. "We paid over a million three years ago, and half again just in taxes."

G. W. whistled. "That's a helluva bite."

"You're telling me. Dad's sorry we ever got in. He's never gonna retire, anyway."

"What's he do?"

"He's got a TV show."

It turned out their new friend who'd gotten stuck with the expensive Australian cattle ranch he couldn't sell was Jack Linkletter, son of Art.

They parted after sharing breakfast the next morning, and then Emmett and G. W. were on their way back to America without a ranch.

"Good thing we run into that Art fella's son so's he could tell us about them taxes," G. W. said.

Emmett nodded. "Kids say the darnedest things."

Once Emmett returned home, he discovered that a new state highway was being built right through the middle of his land, and the county road commission had been ordered to make him an offer he couldn't refuse—not because it was overly generous but because of a little thing called eminent domain. In spite of all the bribes he'd given out over the years to various county offices in the pursuit of votes and hooch sales, Emmett didn't have a leg to stand on. If he fought, he'd lose. If he agreed, he would at least get fair market value.

For the first time in his life, Emmett was forced to do something he didn't want to do. He made plans to sell his ranch and relocate. He and G. W. had their eye on some property in New Mexico, which suited Merl much better than Australia. Merl was a homebody, and she wanted to at least stay in the country.

Emmett and G. W. planned a trip to look at a motel and trailer park in Questa, which was about thirty miles north of Taos. The owner was down in Dallas the weekend they planned to travel, so they first drove down to Big D to meet him and take care of another errand before continuing on to New Mexico.

There was a fella Emmett knew from his bootlegging days who ran a poker game that he wanted to see in the Oak Cliff section of Dallas.

They met with the owner of the New Mexico property at the Adolphus Hotel downtown and, after a successful negotiation, agreed to terms of the sale conditioned on Emmett's inspection of the property. Afterward, Emmett and G. W. drove across the Trinity River and headed for Oak Cliff to find the restaurant with the illegal poker game in the back. It turned out the game was located just around the corner from the Texas Theatre, where Lee Harvey Oswald had been caught after shooting President Kennedy.

As soon as they walked in, Emmett saw Pete, the man he was looking for. Pete had delivered whiskey for Emmett for about a year before he suddenly disappeared without a trace. Emmett had only heard he was down in Dallas running the poker game a few months before, and he was looking forward to seeing him and maybe winning a little money.

Pete, however, was not looking forward to seeing Emmett, and he fainted dead away as soon as he saw him.

Emmett and G. W. walked over to where Pete had collapsed.

"He didn't seem too happy to see you, Emmett."

"Sure didn't."

"Think he's dead?"

"Don't reckon he's that bad off."

"He just fainted," said a bespectacled man seated at a table nearby, one of the only customers in the place. It was after lunch and before the dinner rush.

Emmett turned to the man, who had already gone back to scribbling in his notepad. "You know Pete?" Emmett asked.

"Not at all," the man said. He looked down at Pete, then back up to Emmett. "But it appears he knows you."

"Go get some water or something, G. W.," Emmett said and sat down next to the fella with the notepad. "You mind?"

"Not at all," the man said again as G. W. went to see about Pete's revival. The man made another note and then looked up at Emmett. "That's quite an effect you have on people," he said.

Emmett chuckled. "Might just be Pete."

The man looked Emmett up and down, then shook his head. "I don't think so," he said. It was an odd thing to say and strangely personal, but something about the man's manner was decidedly nonthreatening, so Emmett didn't mind too much. "You are?"

"Emmett Long." He put out his hand, and the man took it. His hands were definitely not the hands of a working man, at least not one who had worked for many years.

"My friends call me Dutch."

Emmett nodded. "OK, Dutch."

By this time, G. W. was back with a pitcher of water and a bar towel and was kneeling over Pete, who finally woke up and opened his eyes. But as soon as he saw Emmett standing over him, he fainted dead away once more.

"I'll be dogged, Emmett," G. W. said. "What the hell's the matter with him?"

"Nothing I know," Emmett said.

"I'd say he's scared of you, Emmett."

Emmett and G. W. turned to look at Dutch, whose face was open and curious and still nonthreatening. They turned back to Pete, and Dutch went back to writing in his notebook.

The next time they revived Pete, Emmett made sure to stand out of sight so it would be G. W. and Dutch he saw when he opened his eyes.

It worked. Pete did not go down for the count, and when he was steady and seated, Emmett eased into his peripheral vision. "Good to see you, Pete."

Pete nearly jumped out of his skin, but he remained vertical and conscious. "I'm sorry, Emmett, I'm really sorry. I swear I didn't—"

"Hang on a second, Pete," Emmett said.

Pete shut his mouth like a sprung trap.

Emmett studied him a moment while Dutch studied Emmett. "I don't know what you're sorry for, but if I can't remember it, then I can't be too mad about it."

Pete's face went from fear to shock to relief in the span of about two seconds, and then his entire body seemed to relax, and he very nearly spilled down the front of his chair.

"Me and G. W. just stopped by to play a little poker," Emmett said.

Pete stood up and repeatedly smoothed his jacket, almost like he were wiping away the shame of his previous behavior. "Game's at nine, Emmett. Door's in the alley. Knock twice. I'll save a couple of seats."

Emmett nodded. "That'll do."

Pete smiled weakly. "I gotta get back to work," he said. "See you tonight." He rushed off before Emmett could answer.

G. W. looked at his watch. "That's three hours, Emmett. Let's get something to eat." He looked at Dutch. "You want to join us, Mister Dutch?"

Dutch nodded. "Very much. But it's Leonard."

Emmett squinted at him. "Thought you said your name was Dutch."

"Last name's Leonard if you're gonna mister me, but like I said, my friends call me Dutch."

G. W. looked at the notepad. "Whatcha got there, Dutch?"

"Notes."

"Notes for what?"

"A book."

"You write books?" G. W. asked.

"That I do," Dutch said.

"I'll be dogged," G. W. said. "Any I heard of?"

He shrugged. "I don't know," he said. "Maybe."

G. W. thought a moment. "I never heard of no Dutch Leonard."

"Use my real name on the books," he said. "Elmore."

G. W. shook his head. "Never heard of no Elmore Leonard, neither."

They had dinner while they waited for the poker game to start. There was something about Dutch that put them both at ease, in spite of all the questions he asked. He told them about some of the books he'd written, some of which had been made into movies, and Emmett told Dutch some bootlegging stories.

He even told the writer about his friend Choc and that bank robbery down in Texas, which greatly surprised G. W. It wasn't like Emmett to spill the beans about a thing like that.

About a half hour before the poker game started, Dutch stood up to leave. "It was a real pleasure meeting you, Emmett Long."

"You too, Dutch."

Dutch looked him straight in the eye, studying him with that piercing but nonthreatening way he had. "I'm gonna remember you," he said.

After they parted company and it was time to walk around to the alley to gain entry to the poker room, G. W. had a thought. "Hey, Emmett."

"Yeah?"

"You think maybe we'll end up as characters in one of that fella's books?"

Emmett thought about that for a moment. "Never can tell," he said.

CHAPTER 22

Mattie was Emmett's pride and joy. Having a child so late in life, he would often be complimented on his adorable "granddaughter" whenever they were out together, something he always found amusing. He called her Baby the rest of his days, long after she was an adult, and he would have moved heaven and earth to get her whatever she needed. Everybody could tell she was Emmett Long's daughter. Mattie was barrel racing by the age of three and driving as soon as her feet could reach the pedals.

Merl doted on her just as much as Emmett, of course. After they lost their first, neither parent thought they'd have another, so Mattie was a wonderful and welcome surprise. She took after each of them in certain ways. She had the fearless spirit of her father and the giving nature of her mother.

Mattie was certainly her mother's daughter, but she was also Daddy's little girl. A happier family could not be found in all of Comanche County or beyond.

And so Emmett was mindful of the two most important women in his life when he came home one day with the news that they were all moving to New Mexico after he bought a beautiful piece of property, where they'd previously gone on vacation, that they would come to call Cottonwood. They would be one of the few private landowners in Carson National Forest, named for the famous American mountain man Kit Carson. Like Emmett, Kit had been an entrepreneur and a jack-of-all-trades with a restless spirit and a boundless taste for adventure.

"We'll do just fine," he assured them, and as long as they were all together, they both knew it would be true. The property included a motel with about twenty cabins, a general store, and hookups for trailers and RVs, catering to local miners and hardy vacationers in particular. It was twenty acres of the most beautiful country on earth, with a trout pond and a river running right through it.

Always the entrepreneur, Emmett added a recreation center with carnival games and pool tables, all available for the price of a quarter. But if the local kids ran out of quarters or had none to begin with, Emmett always kept a cupful of change to keep them happy.

In the summer, there were miners and campers, and in the winter, there were skiers, but Emmett treated them all like family, and most everyone came back, sometimes booking the cabins a year in advance. Merl and Mattie cooked meals for the permanent tenants and opened the store any time of the day or night for urgent needs.

Whether Mattie was serving up hot food to the miners or running the cash register in the convenience store, she would inevitably turn bright red when the rough men fawned over her, amazed by the adorable little girl who seemed to run the show.

"You're awful cute to be in charge, ain't you, honey?"

"My mama and daddy's in charge."

"You can't fool me, sweetheart. I know a boss when I see one."

Whenever Merl saw that Mattie got too embarrassed by the attention, she'd send her to the kitchen or on some other errand, but she enjoyed the attention her daughter got as much as it made Mattie squirm. Merl continued her flower arranging for local weddings and other events, just as she had back in Cache.

G. W. and Geneva moved out west, too, making the enterprise a real family affair. G. W. built a steakhouse up the road, and Emmett and G. W. always tried to keep the sisters together no matter where they went.

G. W. and Geneva's daughter, Jean, whose life had been saved by heart surgery as a baby, helped Mattie cut down Christmas trees every year in the Carson National Forest, for which the government was paid a dollar a tree. The two girls would venture out once a year and spend several days cutting down trees and dragging them back to Cottonwood across the frozen creek, where the two hotel maids would decorate them and set them up in each cabin.

One year, the creek wasn't completely frozen over, and the cousins fell right through the ice, surprised and laughing. The managed to get themselves out of the frigid water and drag the trees back to Cottonwood, waiting in sheets while their clothes were dried.

And after their clothes were dry, they went back to the forest, chopped some more trees, and this time chose a different place to cross the creek.

But through the ice they fell once more!

Back to the laundry, shivering in the sheets, and back to the forest the little girls ventured.

And then it happened a third time, and every time thereafter. Whether the trees were extra heavy that year or the girls were just growing bigger, that was by far the longest Christmas-tree collection of their entire Christmas-tree-cutting career.

A couple of years after they arrived, Emmett decided it was time to buy a new pickup truck, and he took ten-year-old Mattie along with him to the local dealership. Once they picked out the one they wanted, they went into the manager's office while the paperwork was drawn up.

"Daddy?"

"What is it, Baby?"

"Does our new truck have a radio?"

Emmett looked at the manager, who shook his head. "No, sir, it doesn't," he said.

Emmett turned to Mattie. "You want one with a radio?"

Mattie nodded.

"OK, Baby." Emmett chuckled. "Why don't you take this man out there and pick out one you like." He looked at the manager. "One with a radio."

The manager got up and took Mattie outside. She walked up and down the row of cars until she found a pretty blue truck she liked. A brand-new Chevy with a radio.

After they went back inside and completed the new paperwork, the manager walked the two of them outside. "That's a sweet little girl you got there, Mister Long."

"Don't I know it." He laughed, and when the manager held out the keys, Emmett pointed to Mattie. "Toss 'em to her," he said.

The manager smiled and gave the keys to Mattie, thinking she wanted to carry them over to her daddy herself, but instead she climbed into the driver's seat and drove them both off the lot.

Emmett chuckled when he caught the man's expression in the passenger-side mirror. He looked like he was about to have a heart attack watching a ten-year-old drive off in a brand-new Chevrolet pickup truck.

They listened to the radio all the way home, although the music faded in and out as Mattie drove through the mountain passes. But Emmett didn't mind. All he wanted was to make his Baby happy.

It was an idyllic place to live, but the business side of things was a lot of hard work. There was increasing competition up the highway, and so Emmett was always thinking of ways to increase his profit margin. He bought horses and charged two dollars for trail rides, which Mattie often led. He built another dozen cabins. He put in more amenities.

"I know it's hard," Merl would tell Mattie, "but every day is good."

And it was.

Of course, there was the occasional conflict. As mentioned before, Emmett never went looking for trouble, but trouble often came knocking when he was around.

And once, it even came for Merl.

Emmett's wife was always a calming influence. She was what those down South called "as cool as a cucumber." Merl was rarely ruffled about things; rather, she was a problem solver. Just like Emmett, if there was work to be done, she figured she might as well get to it, since complaining would just make things take longer.

And neither Emmett nor Mattie ever knew Merl to lose her temper—until the day Rose Johnson told her a lie about Emmett.

Rose lived at Cottonwood year round with her husband, who'd just been laid off from his work at the mine outside of town. He handled explosives, a skill that would have served his wife well when she made the mistake of joking with Merl about how Emmett had made a pass at her the night before.

Merl knew it wasn't true and figured Rose was scheming to get a month's free rent or some other compensation, but something about the way she said it rubbed Merl the wrong way, and the last anyone saw of Rose was as she ran screaming down the middle of Highway 38 in the general direction of Colorado.

Her husband came by later to pick up their things, which Merl had conveniently set outside for easy pickup.

Not long after that, Emmett sent Merl and his sister Carmen to Hawaii. "Think maybe you need a little vacation," he said.

Carmen's daughter Delores' husband, Ernie, was stationed at Pearl Harbor, so Emmett knew they would be well taken care of. "You go along, too, Baby," he told Mattie. They all had a wonderful time. Merl even got a little tipsy at the luau, a condition Mattie had never before witnessed. "Don't tell your daddy," Merl said to her daughter.

After that, they didn't have much luck with the next tenant in cabin twelve, either. A biker and his girlfriend rode in later that summer, but they'd barely gotten settled in before they got into a screaming argument outside the store. Emmett came out to see what all the ruckus was just as the biker slapped the woman, knocking her to the ground.

Without a word, Emmett walked up to the muscular man, who was about half his age, and knocked him out with a single punch. Then he went back inside and returned with a wet towel, which he handed to the stunned woman to wipe her face, and she sat down on the porch to await her boyfriend's return to the land of the living.

When the biker woke up a few minutes later, he didn't say a single word, just got on his bike and started it up. Emmett asked his girlfriend if she needed a ride anywhere. She seemed to think about it for a minute, then shook her head and climbed on the bike, and the two of them rode off into the night.

Emmett couldn't abide a man who'd hit a woman.

No matter who it was.

"Maybe you need a trip to Hawaii," Merl teased.

During the oil crisis of 1973, an Iraqi fella passing through stopped by the convenience store and had an unfortunate conversation with Boots, who was sitting on the porch with Mattie.

"Whereabouts you from?" Boots asked, noting the man's accent.

"Iraq," he said.

"Where's that?"

The man spat. "You Americans are all the same. Ignorant."

"Ain't no call—"

"You're soft," he said. "No guts."

"How's that?" Boots asked.

"You're soft, but we make America beg. You need our oil. You need gas."

Emmett stepped outside, having heard the man from inside the store. "Mattie, go with your uncle and feed them chickens."

"We already fed 'em, Emmett," Boots said before seeing the look in Emmett's eyes. "Oh, right. Come on, Mattie, let's go."

Boots walked Mattie around the building toward the chicken coop, but Mattie hung back just long enough to peek around the corner, watching her father chase the Iraqi man south on Highway 38, much like her mother had chased Rose.

Eli, the owner of the Gulf station seven miles away, later told Emmett about a foreign-sounding fella who showed up out of breath, claiming he'd run all the way from Cottonwood, chased by some crazy cowboy.

"Sound like anybody you know, Emmett?" he asked, a big smile on his face.

"I may have heard someone like that talkin' about needing gas."

And then there was the time Emmett and his family were having dinner at G. W.'s steakhouse when one of his motel workers showed up and told him there were some high school kids from Questa causing trouble at the store. He left and found them harassing the clerk, waving some kind of martial arts sticks.

Emmett disarmed all four boys and gave them each a whack or two before breaking each stick over his knee for good measure. When they hassled Mattie at school the next day, the principal called Emmett to come pick her up, but instead, he asked the principal to let her stay in class and bring the boys outside to wait for him.

When Emmett got there, he looked at the juvenile delinquents and pointed to a cemetery atop a nearby hill. "That's where I put folks that mess with my Baby," he said, then turned around and walked back to his truck.

None of the boys ever spoke to or even looked at Mattie again.

Quite a bit of her father's wild side seemed to rub off on Mattie during their time at Cottonwood, and when one of her teachers got fired for teaching sex education, she organized a march from the school and a sit-in at the superintendent's office. Her aunt Geneva, who was a teacher at the high school, tried to convince her to step *out* of line and get herself *in* line, but Mattie refused, and the marchers blocked traffic and basically shut down the entire school for half a day.

The county sheriff had to drive all the way in from Taos to break things up.

Merl was pretty upset with Mattie, but Emmett was a little more understanding.

"I reckon we all got a little rebel in us from time to time," he said. "Sometimes trouble just comes knockin', girl."

CHAPTER 23

Despite advancing in years, Emmett still had the profile of a younger man. He walked upright and briskly. He could also still be menacing when necessary. And there were times when the old Emmett still rose to the occasion, especially if Mattie, or any other vulnerable party, was involved.

As a way of giving back to the people of Cache—and to make a few bucks—Emmett built a small rodeo stadium and held an annual Fourth of July rodeo. It was a major local event, complete with concession stands and a full card of events. The local cowboys always participated, so lots of families attended.

At one such occasion, Emmett was standing near the back of the stands when he heard an outburst of profanity coming from nearby. He also noticed people turning toward the offensive language with alarm and disgust on their faces.

Emmett quickly spotted the offenders: two young soldiers (off duty) in civilian clothes and obviously inebriated. They were sitting on top of a split-rail fence and yelling unacceptable comments. Emmett walked over to them and said quietly, "Boys, this is a family show, so you need to cut out the bad language here."

One of them responded, "What the hell does an old man like you think you can do about it?"

What happened next not only took their breath away but ended their day at the rodeo. As though his youth had suddenly and miraculously returned, Emmett took one quick step, kicked a short two-by-four off the end of the fence, picked it up, and managed to knock both of them right off the fence with a single blow. They were injured to the extent that they had to be taken to the hospital in Lawton by the on-site EMTs.

Shortly thereafter, a local deputy sheriff walked up and asked Emmett if there had been any trouble. Emmett looked at him, shook his head, and said, "No, it's pretty much taken care of." And so, the officer left.

A similar incident occurred a few years later at the same location. Merl, Mattie (who was four at the time), and Emmett were seated in the stands at the rodeo. There were, again, two young soldiers from Fort Sill seated in front them. The young men kept jumping up out of their seats, blocking the Long family's view, especially Mattie's.

Mattie complained to her dad that she couldn't see whenever they jumped up. Emmett twice tapped the young man in front of him on the shoulder and asked them to stay in their seats so that his daughter could see. Twice they ignored his request, and so, again, Emmett picked up a small two-by-four (his favorite weapon, it seems) and bashed them in the backs of their heads.

The soldiers fell to the ground and were also assisted from the area by the EMTs. Emmett then turned to Mattie and asked, "Can you see better now, Baby?" She nodded and thanked her daddy.

After moving to Cottonwood Park, Emmett still maintained a cattle ranch in Cache, Oklahoma, and so he had to commute somewhat frequently between the two venues, which created problems. He was working cattle alone one day when his horse shied from a metal bar protruding from the ground and threw him off. When he hit the ground, Emmett rolled right into the bar and broke his hip.

Without anyone around to assist him, Emmett managed to get back in the saddle and ride back to the stable. Somehow, he was then able to make it to his pickup and drive himself to the hospital. When he got there, he was immediately taken into surgery, where his hip was repaired.

After his recovery was finally complete, though, his doctor visited him and told him, "Emmett, I can't keep patching you up. Don't you think it's 'bout time to get out of the ranching business?"

Emmett agreed, and in 1970, he held his last roundup—the old-fashioned way, herding cattle from horseback. Family and friends shared in the event. Everyone was there: Walter (Boots) Callicott, Clinton Reeves, J. B. Long, Jack Long, "Mexican Pete," Pete Unsell, Kink Sims, Marian Huddleston, John (J. D.) Jake, Dennis Long Jr., Steve Hazlewood, Marvin Crabtree, and Asa Dunnington. They were all aware of the significance of the event, that the end of an era was taking place.

In 1990, Emmett began having chest pains. When the cause was eventually diagnosed, he was told he would have to have open-heart surgery because he had seriously blocked arteries. His situation was critical, especially for a man eighty-six years old.

He came through the operation all right, and soon, his recovery was put to the test. He owned an apartment building not far from the "Rock House," as the family home was called. He was there, resting in a chair in front of the apartment building, when he heard a commotion coming from one of the upstairs apartments.

A gentleman who had recently moved out of that apartment was arguing with the new occupant because he was looking for a golf club that was to be shipped to that address. The lady he was yelling at was trying to tell him the club was in the apartment next door to her, as she had given it to the lady to give to him while she went shopping.

Now the lady that she'd given it to was out shopping, so he would have to wait until she returned. He wasn't hearing her. He wanted his club now!

Emmett asked Mattie to intervene, so she managed to talk him down to the ground floor to explain he would just have to wait. Emmett was just around the corner when the man called Mattie—his Baby—a bitch.

No sooner was the epithet out of his mouth than Emmett hit him with a right uppercut, which knocked him off his feet and down into the parking lot. He landed on his nose, breaking it. Emmett said, "I will not tolerate a man talking to a woman that way, especially not to my daughter."

The guy wiped the blood from his nose and went to call the police. The responding officer was a young man who knew Emmett. He asked, "Has there been some trouble here, Mister Long?"

Emmett said, "No, I think the trouble has gone."

"Well, if you have any more, just call us."

Emmett responded, "Son, I have been taking care of trouble all of my life, but thanks."

As Emmett settled into a domestic, and more tranquil, lifestyle, his shows of strength became less common. In his sixties and seventies, he grew to be less imposing of a man. In his younger years, he had been six foot one and 215 pounds.

Slumped with age, he grew closer to six feet and only 190 pounds—still a big man, but showing his frailty. His glasses were a little thicker, and his once-powerful back was not as strong. But there were still times when the old Emmett rose to the occasion, especially if Mattie or any other vulnerable party was involved.

EPILOGUE

By the time Emmett reached his eighty-ninth year, his health had become a more serious issue. Then there was the night when he got up to check on a noise coming from the front of the house, and he fell and rebroke his hip. He was transported to the hospital and was immediately operated upon. His hip was repaired, and following a short recovery, he was sent home.

A couple of days after going home, though, a large hematoma (about the size of a grapefruit) developed at the point of surgery. When Mattie saw it, she took her dad straight back to Southwestern Medical Center, where she worked as a physical therapist and where the surgery had been performed.

The doctors drained the hematoma and sent him to recovery. He wasn't in recovery long, however, before he suffered a mild stroke and a heart attack. He was placed in intensive care, and the family was called in. But he recovered again and was sent back home to recuperate.

It was in the middle of the night that he had a serious heart attack and was returned to the hospital in an ambulance. He was in a great deal of pain but still conscious. Mattie, Merl, his nephew Jack Long, and Mattie's husband, Joe Bloomquist, gathered at his bedside. Mattie was holding his hand when Emmett opened his eyes and said, through his pain, "Baby, this sure ain't livin.'"

Those were his final spoken words. He closed his eyes and fell into a deep sleep.

Emmett's funeral was held in the gymnasium of Cache High School, a place that housed so many items that had been paid for by Emmett and Merl. Most of the residents of Cache and Lawton were in attendance, as well as family and friends from all over the country. And as was the case at most such occasions, there were lots of Emmett stories, laughter, and tears.

Everybody had a story about Emmett Long, and they sure loved to tell 'em.

Which was ironic, considering that Emmett himself was often a man of few words. Taciturn is what they call it—short and to the point.

Lots of Emmett stories are colorful and exciting and memorable, which is why people still love to talk about the man who grew to be a legend. People were proud to know him, because he was always larger than life, a doer more than a talker. He never left something undone that needed doing or left a job for someone else if he could do it himself. Someone once said that Emmett should have been the subject of one of those *Reader's Digest* articles entitled "My Most Unforgettable Character."

Almost every human being is made up of a mixture of good and of bad, of upright moral standing and temptation to do evil. But rarely has a man lived a life like Emmett's—a life that swung to the extremes of both of those divisions of character.

A bank-robbing outlaw . . . who was a cherished pillar of the community.

Who cheated a greedy poker player or even a "corrupt" banking system out of thousands of dollars . . . and yet never uttered a swear word or tolerated one spoken in his presence.

Who dressed up like a major in the army to sell whiskey and play poker at the Officers' Club (and the officers never knew it!) . . . and yet treated the military men with nothing but the utmost respect.

Who ran with the likes of Pretty Boy Floyd . . . and yet used his fortune to benefit the less fortunate children of his town.

No, the Lord Himself broke the mold when He created Emmett Long, and the world has never been the same since He called one of His favorite rascals back home.

Mourners overflowed the high school gymnasium in Cache, Oklahoma, for the funeral. It rained that morning, which was the kind of weather that Emmett had always loved. Everyone knew he loved thunderstorms, and when Stony Huddleston told the crowd it was a clear sign that Emmett was already up in heaven seeing about the weather, everyone laughed—just as Emmett would have wanted them to.

All kinds of people attended the service. There were business owners and ranchers and people of all colors. There were young and old, rich and poor, even cowboys and Indians. Many of the Comanche families in the area came to pay their respects to the man they'd called *Posah-tai-vo*, which, when translated, means "crazy white man."

Lots of the people at the service shared affectionate stories about Emmett. He was known far and wide as someone who never turned away a person in need, and he never let anyone go hungry. His service was held in the school gymnasium beneath the very electronic scoreboard he'd paid for himself because he wanted the kids from the high school to have whatever they needed.

Emmett Long took care of his family, friends, and neighbors as best he could, and everybody who met him respected him as a man of his word. You always knew where you stood with him, and he was always someone who could be counted on—and maybe that's about the best thing you could say about anyone.

At his service, the Reverend Goode sang "Amazing Grace," one of Emmett's favorites, and played a tape of Roy Acuff singing another, "Great Speckled Bird."

> *When He cometh descending from heaven*
> *On the cloud that He writes in His Word*
> *I'll be joyfully carried to meet Him*
> *On the wings of that great speckled bird.*

That very same melody was later used for another song, this one by a honky-tonk singer named Hank Thompson in a song called "The Wild Side of Life." Hank Thompson inspired the film *Crazy Heart*, about an imperfect man who nonetheless always tried to do the right thing, which earned Jeff Bridges an Academy Award a few years back.

Those two songs, one a great spiritual hymn and the other a nod to the darker paths we sometimes walk, together in harmony kind of sum up the man Emmett Long really was.

He was no saint; like all of us, he was certainly a sinner. But he was also a good man, and he was redeemed, and you can't do much better than that.

ABOUT THE AUTHOR

Asa Dunnington was born June 7, 1939, in Logan, Iowa. His family moved to Southern California when he was four years old. He was raised in El Monte, California (the end of the Santa Fe Trail) and graduated from El Monte High School in 1957. After graduation, he went into the US Army Reserve and served three and a half years as a tanker. He finished his military commitment by serving four years in the US Air Force. He then graduated from Antelope Valley College after completing ten years of night school. Following graduation, he went to work for Mattel, where he worked for five years to become western regional marketing manager. He left Mattel to join the advance team for the presidential campaign of 1972. He was a lead advance man and remained in the Washington, DC, area until 1974. He then worked for several major corporations before retiring in 2012 after fifteen years at Federal Express.

Asa is married to Cheryl, who is his second wife. He has three children and nine grandchildren. His autobiography, *What a Life!*, can be found on Amazon.